CONSUMING

FIRE For FIRE

PRAYERS

For our God is a consuming fire -(Hebrews 12 vs. 29)

Kwaku Boachie (Brother Kay)

Copyright © 2015 by Kwaku Boachie

Cell: 443-975-5303   Email: ookaku55@yahoo.com
Facebook: Kay Boachie
Skype: Kayboachie
YouTube: brother kay
www.freshfireprayer.com

Unless otherwise indicated, all scriptural quotations in this book are from the New King James Version of the Bible (NKJV)

No part of this book may be reproduced or transmitted in any form or by any means without the permission in writing from the author

Published by CT Printing and Graphics
10218 New Hampshire Ave
Silver Spring, MD 20903

Edited and Page Layout by Mr. Joey Ofori and Mrs. Esther Boachie

ISBN: 978-0-9864261-0-0

DEDICATION

I wish to dedicate this book to my Heavenly father who loved me so much that He gave me Jesus Christ to die for my sins and eternal life. I dedicate this book to Jesus Christ, the Anointed One. I give thanks to the person of the Holy Spirit who is my comforter, strength giver, my teacher, guide and the one who gives me the unction to function in my life as a Christian and also in ministry.

I wish to also acknowledge my dear wife Esther Boachie and my children Sony, Sonia and Sarah for their love and support in ministry.

Last but not the least, I wish to dedicate this book to the sons and daughters of Fresh Fire Prayer Ministry for their love and support.

All that I am and all that I will ever become I owe it to Jesus Christ my Lord and Master. I love You because You first loved me.

TABLE OF CONTENTS

INTRODUCTION 1

Chapter 1: The Fire of God 2

Chapter 2: Refiners Fire 8

Chapter 3: Benefits of the Fire of God 12

Chapter 4: Why We Use the Fire of God 26

Chapter 5: God's Fiery Weapons 33

Chapter 6: God is a Consuming Fire 43

Chapter 7: The God Who Answers by Fire..........................52

Chapter 8: Exposed by the Fire of God 62

Chapter 9: Fire 4 Fire Prayers 77

INTRODUCTION

The revelation contained in this book will help you to better understand why we invoke the fire of God in our prayers. It will teach you how and when to use the fire of God in prayers. You will also learn of the benefits the fire of God produces in the life of a Christian.

This book contains fiery prayers that will help you to effectively deal with unfriendly friends and also stubborn enemies who disguise themselves us friends. The prayers contained in this book will expose, disarm, disgrace, and destroy witchcraft and demonic activities that are working against you and your family.

When you fast and pray with the prayers in this book, God will arise on your behalf and cause your enemies to be scattered by His consuming fire. The devil and his agents cannot stand the consuming fire of the Holy Ghost. You will receive your deliverance and miracle by fire as you pray the prayers in this book.

As you get ready to engage in a spiritual warfare battle against the forces of darkness, may God baptize you with His Holy Ghost and fire in Jesus Mighty name. **As you open your mouth to pray the prayers in this book, may the fire of God come out of your mouth and consume all your enemies in Jesus name. Remember, Your God is a consuming fire.**

CHAPTER 1

THE FIRE OF GOD

A fire goes before Him, and burns up His enemies round about. His lightning lights the world; the earth sees and trembles. The mountain melt like wax at the presence of the LORD, at the presence of the Lord of the whole earth. - (Psalm 97 vs. 3 to 5)

Fire has two sides to it in the physical realm. On one side it can be very useful to man when under control and on the other hand when it is out of control it can be very dangerous.

Use of Fire When Under control:
- Cooking
- Energy
- Blacksmithing (for melting metals for tools)
- Landscaping (Clearing weeds)
- Lighting (Torches)
- Communication-Signaling
- Repel predators
- Heating houses

Dangerous Use of Fire:

- Cause burns
- Launch a missile
- Shoot a weapon
- Detonate an explosive
- Burn down house and properties
- Explosives (Atomic and Nuclear bombs)
- Volcanic eruption

In the same vein, the fire of God can be of tremendous blessing to the Christian but very destructive to the enemies of God.

SOURCE OF THE FIRE:
The fire comes from the Godhead, which is made up of God the Father, God the Son and God the Holy Spirit.

GOD THE FATHER:
Fire emanates from God the Father. The glorious presence of God produces fire.

> *And above the firmament over their heads was the likeness of a throne, in appearance like a sapphire stone; on the likeness of the throne was a likeness with the appearance of a man high above it. Also from the appearance of His waist and upwards I saw, as it were, the color of amber with the appearance of fire all around within it; and from the appearance of*

> *His waist and downwards I saw, as it were, the appearance of fire with brightness all around- (Ezekiel 1 vs. 26 to 27)*

This was a vision Ezekiel saw describing God on His throne. God's waist upwards and downwards is full of fire with brightness all around Him. This proves indeed that our God is a consuming fire.

> *For our God is a consuming fire -(Hebrews 12 vs. 29)*

> *For the Lord thy God is a consuming fire, even a jealous God -(Deuteronomy 4 vs. 24)*

> **The LORD talked with you face to face on the mountain from the midst of the fire. -(Deuteronomy 5 vs.4)**

> *So it was, when you heard the voice from the midst of the darkness, while the mountain was burning with fire, that you came near to me, all the heads of your tribes and your elders. And you said: 'Surely the LORD our God has shown us His glory and His greatness, and we have heard His voice from the midst of the fire. -(Deuteronomy 5 vs. 23 to 24)*

This scripture above shows how God revealed Himself to the children of Israel on the mountain as a burning fire.

GOD THE SON:
Jesus Christ is described as a refiners fire.

> *Behold, I send my messenger, and he will prepare the way before me. And the Lord, whom you seek, will suddenly come to his temple, even the Messenger of the covenant, in whom you delight. Behold, He is coming, says the LORD of hosts. But who can endure the day of his coming? And who can stand when He appears? For He is like a refiners fire and like fuller's soap. He will sit as a refiner and a purifier of silver; He will purify the sons of Levi, and purge them as gold and silver, that they may offer to the LORD an offering in righteousness. -(Malachi 3 vs. 1 to 3)*

This scripture is describing the ministry of John the Baptist and Jesus Christ. John the Baptist came to prepare the way for Jesus Christ described as a refiners fire.

> *His head and hair were white like wool, as white as snow, and His eyes like flames of fire. -(Revelation 1 vs.14)*

This is John describing the glory of Jesus Christ in the book of revelation.

> *At midday, O king, along the road I saw a light from heaven, brighter than the sun, shining around me and those who journeyed with me. And when we all had fallen to the ground, I heard a voice speaking to me and saying in the Hebrew language, 'Saul, Saul, why are you persecuting Me? It is hard for you kick against the goads.' So I said, 'Who are You, Lord?' And He said, 'I am Jesus, whom you are persecuting. -(Acts 26 vs. 13 to 15)*

This is when Paul encountered Jesus Christ in His glory on the way to Damascus to persecute the Christians. Jesus Christ fiery glory is far brighter than the sun.

GOD THE HOLY SPIRIT:
The Holy Spirit is also fire according to the Bible.

> *I indeed baptize you with water for repentance. But after me will come one who is more powerful than I, whose sandals I am not fit to carry. He will baptize you with the Holy Spirit and with fire. -(Matthew 3 vs. 11)*

> *When the Day of Pentecost had fully come, they were all with one accord in one place. And suddenly there came a sound from heaven, as of a rushing mighty wind, and it filled the whole house where they were sitting. Then there appeared to them divided tongues, as of fire, and one sat upon each of them. And they were all filled with the Holy Spirit and began to speak with other tongues, as the Spirit gave them utterance. -(Act 2 vs. 1 to 4)*

From what we have discovered from the scriptures, we can conclude that God the Father is a consuming fire, Jesus Christ is fire and the Holy Spirit is also fire. **Our God is indeed a consuming fire.**

CHAPTER 2

REFINERS FIRE

For He is like a refiners fire and like fuller's soap. He will sit as a refiner and a purifier of silver; He will purify the sons of Levi, and purge them as gold and silver, that they may offer to the LORD an offering in righteousness.
-(Malachi 3 vs. 2 to 3)

We have two major types of fire of God. We have the Pentecostal fire of God (Refiners fire) and the judgment fire of God.

The Pentecostal fire of God does not only empower us with the Holy Ghost but also refines us. The refiner's fire of the Holy Ghost comes into our lives to purify us from sin and the works of the flesh. It comes to consume anything in us that is not of God. Just as the refining process of a metal separate the dross from the pure metal, so in the same way the refiners fire of God burns up sins in our lives and present us holy before Almighty God.

But you shall receive power when the Holy Spirit has come upon you; and you shall be witness to Me in Jerusalem, and in all Judea and Samaria, and to the end of the earth. -(Act 1 vs. 8)

FUNCTIONS OF THE PENTICOSTAL FIRE (REFINERS FIRE) OF GOD:
- Symbol of Holy Ghost baptism in our lives
- Empowers us for ministry
- Empowers us to become true children of God.
- Empowers us to walk in the spirit and not in the flesh
- Brings revival to our lives and churches
- Set us on fire for God
- Gives us the enthusiasm or zeal for the things of God
- Gives us the passion for Bible studies, prayers, fasting and service of God
- Burn down the works of the flesh in us: adultery, fornication, uncleanness, lewdness, idolatry, sorcery, hatred, contention, jealousies, outburst of wrath, selfish ambitions, dissensions, heresies, envy, murders, drunkenness, revelries etc.
- It purifies us by giving us the desire to be holy and upright before God
- It consumes evil passions and desires from our lives.

- It consumes destructive addictions from our lives
- It draws us closer to God to experience His glorious presence

PRAYER TOPICS:

1. *Heavenly Father, Let your refiners fire burn into ashes anything in my life which is not of you in Jesus name.*

2. *Send down your refiners fire into my life to purify me from all the works of the flesh in Jesus name.*

3. *In the name of Jesus Christ, I command the refiners fire to burn into ashes every destructive addiction in my life in Jesus name.*

4. *Let the refiner's fire of God purge me from all spiritual laziness in Jesus name.*

5. *In the name of Jesus Christ, I command the refiners fire to burn any lukewarmness I have towards the things of God in my life in Jesus name.*

6. *I command the Pentecostal fire of God to come upon me and set me on fire for Jesus Christ.*

7. *I command my passion for Bible studies, prayers, fasting and holy living to return to me by the refiners fire of God in Jesus name.*

8. *I command my zeal for the services of God to return to me by the refiners fire in Jesus name.*

9. *I command the Pentecostal fire of God to bring revival into my life in Jesus name.*

10. *Heavenly Father, in the Mighty name of Jesus Christ, let your refiners fire enter into my body, soul and spirit and set me ablaze for Jesus.*

The Judgment fire of God on the other hand brings the wrath or anger of God upon God's enemies. God uses His consuming fire to deal with his enemies by burning them up so in the same vein God expect you to learn how to use the consuming fire as a weapon to consume your enemies who rise up against you in Jesus name. The fire of God when applied correctly in faith is a deadly weapon in the hands of the believer. Satan and his cohorts cannot stand the heat generated by the fire of God.

CHAPTER 3

BENEFITS OF THE FIRE OF GOD

Our God shall come, and shall not keep silence: a fire shall devour before him, and it shall be very tempestuous round about him.
-(Psalm 50:3)

The fire of God comes with great benefits to the child of God who knows how to invoke it through the medium of prayers.

BENEFITS OF THE FIRE OF GOD:
- **Divine protection from evil**
- **Weapon of judgment on God's enemies**
- **Manifest the glorious presence of God**
- **To guide the children of God**
- **Empowers the children of God**

DIVINE PROTECTION:
You can invoke the fire of God in prayers to protect you and your family from all your enemies and their diabolic plans against you in Jesus name. The fire of God can separate you from your enemies so that they cannot touch you.

> *Now it came to pass, in the morning watch, that the LORD looked down upon the army of the Egyptians through the pillar of fire and clouds, and He troubled the army of the Egyptians. And He took off their chariots wheels, so that they drove them with difficulty; and the Egyptians said, " Let us flee from the face of Israel, for the LORD fights for them against the Egyptians. –(Exodus 14 vs. 24 to 25)*

God troubled the Egyptians with dreadful thunders and lightning with flashes of fire to scare them off. When you invoke the fire of God in your prayers for protection it will scare off your enemies who are pursuing after you in Jesus name.

PRAYER POINTS:

- **Heavenly Father, in the Mighty name of Jesus Christ, send down your consuming fire to trouble my enemies who are pursuing me in Jesus name.**

- **Let the consuming fire of God burn into ashes of evil pursuers of my dream and visions in Jesus name.**

The fire of God also protected Elisha and his servant from their enemies. The Bible says that after the King of Syria found out that Elisha the prophet was the one who was leaking his plans against Israel to the King of Israel, the King of Syria decided to have him arrested and killed by his great army. He knew that if he could get rid of Elisha, then it would be easy for him to defeat the nation of Israel.

The Bible declares:
Therefore, the heart of the king of Syria was greatly troubled by this thing; and he called his servants and said to them, "Will you not show me which of us is for the king of Israel?" And one of his servants said, "None my Lord, O king; but Elisha, the prophet who is in Israel, tells the king of Israel the words that you speak in your bedroom." So he said, "Go and see where he is, that I may send and get him." And it was told him, saying, "Surely he is in Dothan." Therefore he sent horses and chariots and a great army there, and they came by the night and surrounded the city. And when the servant of the man of God arose early and went out, there was an army, surrounding the city with horses and chariots. And his servant said to him, "Alas, my master! What shall we do?" So he (Elisha) answered, do not fear, for those who are with us are more than those who are with them."

And Elisha prayed, and said, LORD, I pray, open his eyes that he may see." Then the LORD opened the eyes of the young man, and he saw. And behold, the mountain was full of horses and chariots of fire all around Elisha. - (2 Kings 6:11-17)

As a child of God, you don't have to be intimidated by evil forces against you because you are never alone. Invoke God's divine protection in your life. Tell your Heavenly Father to surround you and your family with horses and chariots of fire for divine protection in Jesus name.

PRAYER TOPICS:

1. Heavenly Father, In the Mighty name of Jesus Christ, I ask you to deploy your horses and chariot of fire to protect me and my family from all demonic and witchcraft attacks.

2. In the Mighty name of Jesus Christ, Let the horses and chariot of fire surround my house or apartment and protect me from every satanic attack in Jesus name.

3. Let the horses and chariot of fire protect my going out and coming in in Jesus name.

4. Let the chariot of fire encamp around me everywhere I go in Jesus name.

5. In Jesus name, let your horses and chariot of fire protect me when I sleep and protect my dreams from all demonic and witchcraft attacks against me.

6. I command the horses and chariot of fire to protect my family and my marriage from demonic attacks in Jesus name.

7. In the Mighty name of Jesus, I command the horses and chariot of fire to protect my vehicle from accidents.

8. I command the horses and chariot of fire to protect my spouse, children, health, business, and job from all the attacks of the enemy in Jesus name.

WEAPON OF JUDGMENT ON GOD'S ENEMIES:

For we do not wrestle against flesh and blood, but against principalities, against powers, against the rulers of the darkness of this age, against spiritual host of wickedness in the heavenly places.
–(Ephesians 6 vs. 12)

As believers we have to understand that our enemy is the devil and his agents. The devil and his agents come only to steal, kill and destroy. As a believer of Jesus Christ, **if you want to have victory over satanic attacks in your life, then you have to fight the powers of darkness through the word of God and spiritual warfare prayers.**

Satanic Hierarchy:
- **Satan**
- **Principalities**
- **Powers**
- **Rulers of Darkness**
- **Host of wickedness in heavenly places**

When we invoke the judgment fire of God in our prayers against our enemies, the anger of God is kindled against them. Invoke the fire of God in your prayers against the forces of darkness mentioned above. Use the fire of God in spiritual warfare prayers to destroy the strongman and strongwoman in your life. Command the judgment fire of God in your prayers to destroy every plans, devices, schemes, plot, conspiracies, intentions, expectation, and imaginations against you and your family in Jesus name.

MANIFEST GOD'S GLORIOUS PRESENCE:
Throughout the scripture, we find God manifesting His presence in the form of fire. He appeared to Moses in a

burning bush of fire and also to children of Israel on Mountain Sinai as a fire.

And the Angel of the LORD appeared to him in a flame of fire from the midst of the bush. So he looked, and behold, the bush was burning with fire, but the bush was not consumed. Then Moses said, " I will now turn aside and see this great sight, why the bush does not burn. -(Exodus 3 vs. 2 to 3)

> *And Moses brought the people out of the camp to meet with God, and they stood at the foot of the mountain. Now Mount Sinai was completely in smoke, because the LORD descended upon it in fire. Its smoke ascended like the smoke of a furnace, and the whole mountain quaked greatly. -(Exodus 19 vs. 17 to 18)*

> *Then you came near and stood at the foot of the mountain, and the mountain burned with fire to the midst of heaven, with darkness, cloud, and thick darkness. And the LORD spoke to you out of the midst of the fire. You heard the sound of the word, but saw no form; you only heard a voice. -(Deuteronomy 4 vs. 11 to 12)*

The glorious presence of God was manifested in the form of fire whenever God was pleased with an offering or sacrifice offered to Him in worship by His children.

Example: Solomon
When Solomon had finished praying, fire came down from heaven and consumed the burnt offering and the sacrifice; and the glory of the LORD filled the temple. And the priest could not enter the house of the LORD, because the glory of the LORD had filled the LORD's house. When all the children of Israel saw how the fire came down, and the glory of the LORD on the temple, they bowed their faces to the ground on the pavement, and worshipped and praised the LORD, saying: For He is good, For His mercies endures forever. – (2 Chronicles 7 vs. 1 to 3)

Example: Aaron and Moses
Then Aaron lifted his hand toward the people, blessed them, and came down from offering the sin offering, the burnt offering, and peace offerings. And Moses and Aaron went into the tabernacle of meeting, and came out and blessed the people. Then the glory of the LORD appeared to all the people, and fire came out from before the LORD and consumed the burnt offering and the fat on the altar. When all the people saw it, they shouted and fell on their faces. -(Leviticus 9 vs. 22 to 24)

God has not changed. He is the same God yesterday, today and forever more. If you and I will worship and praise Him in truth and in spirit, we will see His Shekinah glory revealed to us.

PRAYER TOPICS:

- *Heavenly father, in the Mighty name of Jesus Christ, I offer by body, soul, and spirit to you as a living sacrifice holy and acceptable to you in Jesus name.*

- *In the Mighty name of Jesus Christ, any sin in my life that is contaminating, polluting, and defiling me from being acceptable to God, let it be purified by the refiner's fire of the Holy Ghost in Jesus name.*

- *Heavenly father, I want to see your Shekinah glory in my life. Let your glory manifest in my life in every thing I do and follow me everywhere I go in Jesus name.*

TO GUIDE THE CHILDREN OF GOD:
The fire of God served as a guide to the children of God when they left Egypt to the promise land. God directed His children by the pillar of fire by night. Today, the Holy Spirit guides us in all our ways.

Who went in the way before you to search out a place for you to pitch your tents, to show you the way you should go, in the fire by night and in the clouds by day. -(Deuteronomy 1 vs. 33)

> *And the LORD went before them by day in a pillar of cloud to lead the way, and by night in a pillar of fire to give them light, so as to go by day and night. He did not take away the pillar of cloud by day or the pillar of fire by night from before the people. -(Exodus 13 vs. 21 to 22)*

> *However, when He the Spirit of truth, has come, He will guide you into all truth; for He will not speak on His own authority; but whatever He hears He will speak; and He will tell you things to come. -(John 16 vs. 13)*

EMPOWERS THE CHILDREN OF GOD:
The baptism of the Holy Ghost firepower gives the Christian the ability to become a true child of God. It gives you the zeal and passion to serve God with all your heart, soul and mind.

> *I baptize you with water for repentance. But after me will come one who is more powerful than I, whose sandals I am not fit to carry. He*

will baptize you with the Holy Spirit and with fire. -(Matthew 3 vs. 11)

But as many as received Him, to them He gave the power to become sons of God, even to them that believe on his name. -(John 1 vs. 12 KJB)

Behold I give you authority to trample on serpents and scorpions, and over all the powers of the enemy, and nothing shall by any means hurt you. -(Luke 10 vs. 19)

God makes His servants or ministers flames of fire to carry out His purposes on earth.

Who makes His angels spirits, His ministers a flame of fire. -(Psalm 104 vs. 4)

Then I said," I will not make mention of Him, nor speak anymore in His name." But His word was in my heart like a burning fire shut up in my bones. -(Jeremiah 20 vs. 9)

And I will give power to my two witnesses, and they will prophesy one thousand two hundred and sixty days, clothed in sackcloth. These are the two olive trees and the two lampstands standing before the God of the earth. And if anyone wants to harm them, fire proceeds out from their mouth and devours their enemies. And if anyone wants to harm them, he must be killed in this manner. -(Revelation 11 vs. 3 to 5)

God has given you and I power to overcome the powers of darkness and also live for His glory. It is time you and I begin to walk in the power and the authority God has given to us in Jesus name.

PRAYER TOPICS:

1. *Heavenly father I ask you to baptize me afresh with your fire and your power anointing in Jesus name.*

2. *In Jesus Mighty name, I receive the firepower anointing by faith to do exploits this year in Jesus name.*

3. *In the Mighty name of Jesus Christ, I receive the firepower anointing to trample over scorpions and serpents in Jesus name.*

4. *Heavenly father, let me be on fire for Jesus.*

5. *Heavenly Father, anoint my tongue and mouth with your fire to preach your word with power in Jesus name.*

6. *Heavenly Father, anoint my heart with your fire to love you with all my heart, soul and mind in Jesus name.*

7. *Heavenly Father, in Jesus name, anoint my hands with your fire to heal the sick and cast out demons from people in Jesus name.*

8. *Heavenly Father, anoint my whole body with your Holy Ghost fire to perform signs and wonders in the Mighty name of Jesus Christ.*

9. *Heavenly Father, anoint my body with your Holy Ghost fire to repel every dark powers in Jesus name.*

10. *Let the Holy Ghost fire burn within me to serve God in spirit and in truth in Jesus name.*

11. *Let the Holy Ghost fire burn within me to pray fervently in Jesus name.*

12. *Let the fire of God burn within me to read my Bible consistently in Jesus name.*

13. *Lord set me ablaze for Jesus Christ to witness the gospel to family members and friends without fear in Jesus name.*

14. I command the Pentecostal fire of revival to come upon me in Jesus name.

15. Let the fire of God enter into my body, soul and spirit in Jesus name.

16. Let the fire of revival burn up every sin from my life and purify me in Jesus name.

17. I receive the firepower anointing to trample over witches and wizards fighting against me in life in Jesus name.

18. I receive the firepower anointing, to subdue all my enemies under my foot in Jesus name.

19. In the Mighty name of Jesus Christ, I receive the firepower anointing to preach the gospel of Jesus Christ with boldness and power in Jesus name.

CHAPTER 4

WHY WE USE THE FIRE OF GOD

When He had come to the other side, to the country of the Gergesenes, there met Him two demon-possessed men, coming out of the tombs, exceedingly fierce, so that no one could pass that way. And suddenly they cried out, saying, " What have we to do with You, Jesus, You Son of God? Have You come here to torment us before the time?
-(Matthew 8 vs. 28 to 29)

Demons and all evil spirits do not like to be tormented. In fact, the spirit of witchcraft and demons operate very well where the judgment fire of God is absent. Witchcraft and demonic spirit can be working against you for a very long time undetected if the fire of God is not present to smoke them out of their hideouts.

> *When an unclean spirit goes out of a man, he goes through dry places, seeking rest; and finding none, he says, ' will return to my house from which I came.'- (Luke 11 vs. 24)*

Demon and witchcraft spirit are seeking rest in their victims. They don't want their victims to resist them. They want comfort and rest to operate their diabolic activities against people. As a Christian, you don't have to give the devil and his demons rest or comfort. You have to torment them constantly with the fire of God in your prayers until they leave you alone.

WHO CAN USE THE FIRE OF GOD IN PRAYERS:

It is important for us to understand that until you are born again believer, you do not have access to these lethal weapon of the fire of God. This weapon of warfare is for children of the kingdom.

The Bible says that unto the children of God only is it given to know the mysteries of the kingdom of God. Unto others, they are parables. People who have received Jesus as their Lord and personal savior and are filled with the Holy Ghost power can only use it. It must also be noted here that part-time Christians will not see the effectiveness of this weapon of warfare. **It is deadly and effective weapon in the hands of full-time Christians; people who have dedicated their life fully to follow Jesus.** This is what happens if you are not a child of God and you try to use these lethal weapons against the devil and his cohorts.

The Bible declares:
> *Now God worked unusual miracles by the hands of Paul, so that even handkerchiefs or aprons were brought from his body to the sick, and the disease left them and the evil spirit went out of them. Some of the itinerant Jewish exorcists took it upon themselves to call the name of the Lord over those who had evil spirits, saying, "We exorcise you by the Jesus whom Paul preaches." Also there were seven sons of Sceva, a Jewish chief priest, who did so. And the evil spirit answered and said, "Jesus I know, and Paul I know; but who are you?" Then the man in whom the evil spirit was leaped on them, overpowered them, and prevailed against them, so that they fled out of that house naked and wounded. - (Acts 19:11-16)*

If you are not a serious Christian and you begin to release fire against the devil and his demonic spirit, there will be backlash against you.

The first step to take to walk in power and dominion in Jesus name is to become born-again. When you become born-again Christian, then you can effectively use the fire against your enemies in Jesus name. To become a born-again Christian means to receive the Lord Jesus Christ into your heart and life as your Lord and personal savior.

The Bible declares, Therefore, just as through one man sin entered the world, and death through sin, and thus death spread to all men, because all sinned.
- (Romans 5 vs. 12)

For all have sinned and fall short of the glory of God.
- (Romans 3 vs. 23)

As it is written: There is none righteous, no, not one.
- (Romans 3 vs. 10)

Above scriptures prove that we are all born sinful and none of us is innocent before God.

What is Sin?
Sin simply means missing God's mark or righteous standards. Sin is breaking of God's Law or commandments and rebelling or disobeying against God's will.

> *Whoever commits sin also commits lawlessness, and sin is lawlessness.*
> *- (1 John 3 vs. 4)*

What Happens to Sinners?
The Bible declares:
> *The soul who sins shall die. - (Ezekiel 8 vs. 20)*

> *For the wages of sin is death; but the gift of God is eternal life through Jesus Christ our Lord. - (Romans 6 vs. 23)*

These scriptures show that sinners will face the judgments of God.

How to Become Saved or a Born-Again Christian:

> **For God so loved the world that He gave His only begotten Son, that whoever believes in Him should not perish but have everlasting life. – (John 3 vs. 16)**

> *For whoever shall call upon the name of the Lord shall be saved. - (Romans 10 vs. 13)*

> **Behold, now is the acceptable time; behold now is the day of salvation. – (2 Corinthians 6 vs. 2)**

To become saved or a born-again Christian, you have to believe in the Lord Jesus Christ, receive Him into your heart, and repent from all your sins.

The Bible declares:

> **If you confess with your mouth the Lord Jesus and believe in your heart that God has raised**

Him from the dead, you will be saved. For with the heart one believes unto righteousness, and with the mouth confession is made unto salvation. - (Romans 10 vs. 9 – 12)

Salvation Prayers:

Heavenly Father, I ask for your forgiveness for all my sins. I accept that I am a sinner and I need Your Son Jesus Christ to forgive me from all my sins.

I receive Jesus Christ into my heart as my Lord and personal savior today. I believe that Jesus Christ died for my sins and You raised Him up from the dead.

Lord Jesus, I thank you for coming into my life. I give my body, soul, and spirit to You. Today, I put my trust in You Amen and amen.

If you prayed this prayer sincerely from your heart, then you are now a born-again Christian. Only believe and the Holy Spirit will help you and lead you into all truth in the Bible. You are now a new creature.

Therefore, if anyone is in Christ, he is a new creature; old things have passed away; behold all things have become new. -(2 Corinthians 5 vs. 17)

You are now ready to enjoy all the benefits of using the fire of God in your daily prayers.

CHAPTER 5

GOD'S FIERY WEAPONS

For the weapons of our warfare are not carnal but mighty in God for pulling down strongholds, casting down arguments and every high thing that exalts itself against the knowledge of God, bringing every thought into captivity to the obedience of Christ.
-(2 Corinthians 10 vs. 4 to 5)

GOD'S FIERY WEAPONS:
- Hail and fire mixed
- Brimstone (Sulfur) and fire mixed
- Live coal
- Burning wind
- Fire from heaven

Hail and Fire mixed:
God used this fiery weapon to bring judgment on Pharaoh and the Egyptians when Pharaoh held the nation of Israel in bondage and slavery.

So there was Hail, and Fire mingled with the Hail, so very heavy that there was none like it in all the land of Egypt since it became a nation. -(Exodus 9 vs. 24)

PRAYER TOPICS:

1. ***In the Mighty name of Jesus Christ, I unleash the judgment of hail and fire against every strongman/strongwoman who has turned my glory upside down in Jesus name.***

2. *I release the judgment of hail and fire to burn into ashes every principalities, powers, rulers of darkness, spiritual host of wickedness in heavenly places, demons and witchcraft spirit fighting against me in Jesus name. I command them to catch fire and die in my life in Jesus name.*

3. ***I call down hail and fire of God to fall upon the heads of witches and wizards frustrating my life and family in Jesus name.***

4. *I unleash the weapon of hail and fire to consume all the evil plans and plots of my enemies against me in Jesus name.*

5. *I call down hail and fire of God to consume into ashes the coven and all the meeting places of my enemies in Jesus name.*

6. *I torment my enemies with God judgment of hail and fire in Jesus name.*

Brimstone (Sulfur) and fire mixed:

God used this weapon to bring judgment upon Sodom and Gomorrah when they rebelled against Him. It is the same weapon that will be used to judge the devil and his false prophets in the end time.

> *Then the LORD rained brimstone and fire on Sodom and Gomorrah, from the LORD out of the heavens. - (Genesis 19 vs. 24)*

> *And the devil, who deceived them, was cast into the lake of fire and brimstone where the beast and the false prophets are. And they will be tormented day and night forever and ever. - (Revelation 20 vs. 10)*

PRAYER TOPICS:

1. *In the Mighty name of Jesus Christ, I call down the brimstone and fire of God to burn*

into ashes every witchcraft activities that are operating against my life and marriage in Jesus name.

2. *I command the brimstone and fire to consume into ashes every attack of witchcraft against my finances and business in Jesus name.*

3. *I command the brimstone and fire of God to come down and burn into ashes every spells, charm, hexes, witchcraft, obeah, Santeria, and voodoo operating against my body in Jesus name.*

4. *I direct the brimstone and fire of God to rain down upon the witches and wizards in their coven in Jesus name.*

5. *I command the brimstone and fire of God to locate all my enemies and rain upon them to destroy all their evil assignment against me and my household in Jesus name.*

6. *I unleash the sulfur fire of God to torment every agent and messenger of satan assigned to destroy me in Jesus name.*

7. *I unleash the sulfur fire of God to burn into ashes every monitoring spirit, monitoring*

agents, and satanic spy monitoring my daily activities in Jesus name.

Live Coal:
God uses coals of fire to bring judgment to his enemies.

Upon the wicked He will rain coals, fire and brimstone and a burning wind; this shall be their portion of their cup. -(Psalm 11 vs. 6)

PRAYER TOPICS:

1. *In the Mighty name of Jesus Christ, I command the judgment coals of fire of God to rain upon the heads of all the wicked spirits that have risen against me in judgment in Jesus name.*

2. *I release the coals of fire to burn down the coven of the witches and wizards attacking me and my family in Jesus name.*

3. *I unleash the coals of fire to rain down on the head of every wicked agent monitoring my life and destiny in Jesus name.*

4. *I command the coals of fire of God to fall upon the heads of household witchcraft fighting me from my mother's bloodline in Jesus name.*

5. *In the Mighty name of Jesus Christ, I command the coal of fire to fall upon the heads of household witchcraft fighting my life and destiny from my father's bloodline in Jesus name.*

6. *In the Mighty name of Jesus Christ, let the coal of fire of God scatter every satanic meetings that is taking place against me in Jesus name.*

Burning Wind:
The burning wind of fire is also another weapon used by God to bring judgment against His enemies.

> *Upon the wicked He will rain coals, fire and brimstone and a burning wind; this shall be their portion of their cup. -(Psalm 11 vs. 6)*

PRAYER TOPICS:

1. *In the Mighty name of Jesus Christ, I command the burning wind of fire to consume into ashes every stealing spirit that has been robbing me of*

my possessions in Jesus name. I command you to die by fire in Jesus name.

2. I command the burning wind of fire to burn into ashes every witchcraft attacks on my health in Jesus name.

3. In Jesus name, I command the burning wind fire of God to consume into ashes every killing demon that has been killing good things in my life. I command you to die by fire in Jesus name.

4. Every agent of darkness troubling me in my marriage, I command the burning wind to drive you out of my marriage in Jesus name.

5. Let the burning wind of God drive out every witch and wizards operating against me at my work place in Jesus name.

6. In the Mighty name of Jesus Christ, I command the burning wind fire of God to consume into ashes every destructive demon that has been send to destroy my marriage, family, spouse, children, business, job, and my destiny. Let the destructive demon die by fire in Jesus name.

7. In the Mighty name of Jesus Christ, I command the burning wind fire of God to drive out of my

work place every witch sent to frustrate me in Jesus name.

8. Every agent assigned to destroy my children; I command the burning wind of fire to drive you far away from my children in Jesus name.

9. I command the burning wind of fire to burn into ashes every witchcraft spells that has been done against my spouse and children in Jesus name.

10. Every satanic agent assigned against my spouse to destroy my marriage, I command the burning wind of fire to burn you out of my spouse life in Jesus name.

11. Let the burning wind of God drive out every witch and wizard operating against my family in Jesus name.

12. I command the burning wind of fire to burn into ashes every witchcraft that has been done against my marriage in Jesus name.

13. I command the burning wind of fire to burn into ashes every witchcraft attack on my finances in Jesus name.

Fire From Heaven:
The servant of God, Elijah used the fire from heaven to destroy his enemies.

> *So Elijah answered and said to them "If I am a man of God, let fire come down from heaven and consume you and your fifty men. "And the fire of God came down from heaven and consumed him and his fifty. - (2 Kings 1 vs. 12)*

PRAYER TOPICS:

1. **If I be a child of God, then I command the consuming fire of God to come down from heaven and burn into ashes every satanic agents working against my success, promotion, vision, prosperity, breakthrough, goals, dreams, happiness, joy, and peace in Jesus name.**

2. **If I be a child of God, then I command the consuming fire of God come down from heaven and consume into ashes every satanic padlocks, chains, shackles, roadblocks, and obstacles put in place to prevent me from achieving my goals and dreams in life in Jesus name.**

3. *If I be a child of God, then let fire come down from heaven and consume into ashes every evil plans, programs, expectations, prediction and projection against my health, finances, job, marriage, family, and children in Jesus name.*

4. *If I be a child of God, then I command the judgment fire of God to come down from heaven and consume into ashes every evil altar erected for my destruction, every false prophet pronouncing curses on me and my family, every divination, incantation, and charm against me and my family, every agent monitoring my progress in life. Let them receive the judgment fire of God in Jesus name.*

5. *If I be a child of the Most High God, then I command the consuming fire of the Holy Ghost to burn into ashes every spirit of set back, delay, stagnation, retrogression, backwardness, lateness and postponing that is preventing me from moving forward in life in Jesus name.*

CHAPTER 6

GOD IS A CONSUMING FIRE

For the Lord thy God is a consuming fire, even a jealous God.
- (Deuteronomy 4:24)

For our God is a consuming fire. -(Hebrews 12:29)

The consuming fire aspect of God reveals the judgment and vengeance side of our God against His enemies. When you invoke the Holy Ghost fire in your prayers, you are calling on the vengeance, wrath, fury, anger, and judgment of God upon your enemies.

Remember that our enemies are not flesh and blood. As believers we are not fighting against humans but demonic spirits without bodies. We are fighting against dark fallen angels or demonic spirits who are either working directly against us or indirectly using people around us to destroy God's purpose in our lives.

> *For we do not wrestle against flesh and blood, but against principalities, against powers, against the rulers of the darkness of this age, against spiritual host of wickedness in the heavenly places. –(Ephesians 6 vs. 12)*

Whenever God moves, His consuming fire go ahead of Him to destroy His enemies. Whenever you invoke the fire of God in your prayers concerning any problem, His fire melts down any problems you present to Him.

> *A fire goes before him, and burns up his enemies round about. His lightning's enlightened the world: the earth saw, and trembled. The hills melted like wax at the presence of the LORD, at the presence of the Lord of the whole earth. -(Psalm 97: 3-5)*

God has enemies so in the same way; if you call yourself a child of God you will also have enemies. As a born-again believer of Jesus Christ, God's enemies become your enemies and your enemies are also God's enemies. God uses His consuming fire to deal with His enemies by burning them up so in the same vein God expect you to learn how to use the consuming fire as a weapon to consume your enemies who rise up against you in Jesus name. It must be noted here that the consuming fire of God or judgment fire of God is a lethal weapon against the devil and demons. Whenever

Consuming Fire for Fire

you invoke the judgment fire of God against your enemies in your prayers, you are sure of total victory over them. The fire of God will consume all their evil plans and programs concerning you. When you invoke the judgment fire of God in warfare prayers, every satanic altar erected for your destruction is burnt down into ashes. When the consuming fire of God is directed at the cabinet meeting place of your enemies, it suffocates the witches and wizards and scatters them. The fire of God when applied correctly in faith is a deadly weapon in the hands of the believer. Satan and his cohorts cannot stand the heat generated by the fire of God.

When you invoke the consuming fire of God in your prayers, it burns up into ashes every witchcraft, hexes, voodoo, Santeria, obeahs curses, incantation, sorceries, divination, and spells that have been programed against you for destruction. It consumes them into ashes and destroys them from operating against you. When you invoke the consuming fire of God in your prayers against your enemies, it set your enemies on fire. Your enemies begin to experience the heat of the fire and it torments them day and night. It stops the demons, witches, wizards, strongman/strongwoman, spirit husband/wife, leviathan spirit, python spirit, familiar spirit, monitoring spirits, and all the occultic powers from operating their evil against you. The consuming fire of God also melt up like wax every witchcraft and demonic orchestrated problems from the pit of hell that is sent into your life to frustrate you. **Many of the problems people face on daily bases are not normal but are engineered by witches and wizards to destroy and frustrate them.** When you invoke the consuming fire of God against your problems, the fire melt the problem away. It destroys the evil intention behind the problem and it removes the problem from your life without allowing the problem to destroy you. Every problem melts like wax at the presence of God's fire. The Bible says, "The hills melted like wax at the presence of the LORD, at the presence of the Lord of the whole earth."

And in the greatness of Your excellence, You have overthrown those who rose against You; You sent forth Your wrath; It consumed them like stubble. -(Exodus 15 vs. 7)

God's anger is unleashed against those who oppose Him by consuming them into ashes by His fire. You can also release the consuming fire of God to burn into ashes every spirit that rise up against your progress in life. You can invoke the fire of God to consume into ashes every opposing spirits delaying your miracle and breakthrough from manifesting in your life this year. When you use the fire of God, the wrath of God is directed against the obstacles to your miracles and they are reduced into ashes by the consuming fire of God.

> *Therefore we wanted to come to you even I, Paul, time and again-but Satan hindered us.*
> *-(1 Thessalonians 2 vs. 18)*

> *For a great and effective door has opened to me, and there are many adversaries.*
> *-(1 Corinthians 16 vs. 9)*

Apostle Paul was experiencing fierce opposition even though a great and effective door was open to him. There were times these opposing forces stopped him from moving forward with the work of God. The best way to deal with these adversaries is to command the fire of God to consume them into ashes. When invoke the fire of God in your prayers all satanic roadblocks, barricades, embargos, resistances, hindrance, limitations, opposition, and blockages are burnt down into ashes. Once they are consumed into ashes, then you begin to see your miracle and breakthrough manifesting in your life.

Remember that, without removing the obstacles in your life, you cannot see your miracles.

> *Hear, O Israel: You are to cross over the Jordan today, and go into to dispossess nations greater and mightier than yourself, cities great and fortified up to heaven, a people great and*

> *tall, the descendants of the Anakims, whom you know, and of whom you heard it said, ' Who can stand before the descendants of Anak?' Therefore understand today that the Lord your God is He goes over before you as a consuming fire. He will destroy them and bring them down before you; so you shall drive them out and destroy them quickly, as the Lord has said to you. (Deuteronomy 9 vs. 1 to 3)*

The consuming fire of God helps you to deal with strong stubborn enemies who are in possession of your blessings. The fire of God dispossesses them and delivers into your hands your possession. Whenever you are dealing with a strongman/strongwoman in your life that is blocking you from fulfilling your dreams and vision in life, you need to start invoking the consuming fire against them in aggressive prayers. Victory is easily won when the consuming fire of God is used in prayers against evil strongman and woman in prayers. Stubborn problems disappear from your life when God fight for you through His consuming fire. The consuming fire of God exterminates your enemies who plan to destroy and stop you from fulfilling your destiny on earth.

HOW GOD JUDGE EVIL PEOPLE WITH HIS CONSUMING FIRE:

The Bible declares:
Our God shall come, and shall not keep silence: a fire shall devour before him, and it shall be very tempestuous round about him. - (Psalm 50:3)

> *And the LORD said, because the cry of Sodom and Gomorrah is great, and because their sin is very grievous... -(Genesis 18:20)*

> *Then the Lord rained upon Sodom and upon Gomorrah brimstone and fire from the LORD out of heaven; and he overthrew those cities, and all the plain, and all the inhabitants of the cities, and that which grew upon the ground. - (Genesis 19:24-25)*

And when the people complained, it displeased the LORD: and the LORD heard it, and his anger was kindled; and the fire of the LORD burnt among them, and consumed them that were in the uttermost parts of the camp. And the people cried unto Moses; and when Moses prayed unto the LORD, the fire was quenched. - (Numbers 11:1-2)

PRAYER TOPICS:

1. *In the Mighty name of Jesus Christ, I command the consuming fire of God to go ahead of me and scatter my enemies in Jesus name.*

2. *I command the unquenchable fire of God to penetrate the covens and all the meeting places of my enemies and scatter them all in Jesus name.*

3. *Heavenly Father, You are a consuming fire. I ask you to arise on my behalf and scatter all my enemies by your consuming fire in Jesus name.*

4. *Wherever my enemies will meet and plan and plot evil against me and my family let them be scattered by the fire of God in Jesus name.*

5. *Wherever people will mention my name for voodoo, witchcraft, obeah, spells, curses and any evil works, let them be scattered by the consuming fire of God in Jesus name.*

6. *Any demon or agent who has gone ahead of me to block me of my breakthrough, miracles, and blessings this year, let them be scattered by the fire of God in Jesus name.*

7. I release the sulfur fire of God to scatter all evil meetings taken against me in the coven of my enemies in Jesus name.

8. Let the brimstone fire of God chase away my enemies who were pursuing after me in my dreams in Jesus name. Let them flee from my very face now in Jesus name.

9. Let the hot wind of fire of God chase away every demons, witch and agent of darkness send to do me and my family harm in Jesus name. Let them flee before my very face now in Jesus name.

10. In the name of Jesus Christ, I command every strongman/strongwoman responsible for all my problems in life to perish and die by the fire of god in Jesus name.

11. I command the judgment fire of God to destroy every dark power assigned against me and my family in Jesus name.

CHAPTER 7

THE GOD WHO ANSWERS BY FIRE

Then you call on the name of your gods, and I will call on the name of the LORD; and the God who answers by fire, He is God. -(1 King 18 vs. 24)

> "Hear me, O LORD, hear me, that this people may know that You are the LORD God, and that You have turned their heart back to You again." Then the fire of the Lord fell and consumed the burnt sacrifice, and the wood and the stones and the dust, and it licked up the water that was in the trench. Now when all the people saw it, they fell on their faces; and they said, The LORD, He is God! The LORD, He is God! -(1 King 18 vs. 37 to 39)

We serve a living God who answers prayers by fire. This means that the God of Elijah answers our prayers speedily and manifests His glory and power in our lives to silence the voice of our accusers. There are times in our lives when people ask question like, " If you say you are a Christian then where is your God? How come your God Has not answered your prayers?

How come you don't have your breakthrough and miracle? How come you don't have this or that?" When people begin to make mockery of you and your God, you have to pray and ask God to answer you by fire and by force to silence your enemies.

The scripture above is about prophet Elijah who single handedly challenged the four hundred and fifty prophets of Baal, and also the four hundred prophets of Asherah. The prophets of Baal believed that their god controlled thunder, lightning, and the storms. **Elijah wanted to prove to them and the children of Israel that there was only one God and His ultimate power controlled the whole world.** So Elijah put them to a test to prove who was the true God. The prophets of Baal and Asherah tried to call down fire to burn their altar but fire did not come. They called upon their Baal the whole day but their god, Baal did not respond. **Then Elijah called upon his God, the God of Israel and fire came down immediately to burn his altar.**

As a child of God, when you invoke the consuming fire of God in your situation, God answers your prayer speedily. You receive speedily your miracles and breakthroughs when the fire of God is invoked in any situation in faith. When the fire of God is invoked in your prayers, it will humiliate and destroys the powers of darkness frustrating your life and destiny in Jesus name.

> *And I will give power to my two witnesses, and they will prophesy one thousand two hundred and sixty days, clothed in sackcloth. These are the two olive trees and the two lampstands standing before the God of the earth. And if anyone wants to harm them, fire proceeds out from their mouth and devours their enemies. And if anyone wants to harm them, he must be killed in this manner. -(Revelation 11 vs. 3 to 5)*

God has given His children the authority and power in the name of Jesus Christ to call down the consuming fire to destroy the powers of darkness against His kingdom on earth.

Elijah knew just how to use the judgment fire of God to deal with his enemies. When King Ahaziah the son of Ahab and Jezebel sent two groups of fifty soldiers to have Elijah arrested, Elijah used the judgment fire of God to defeat them.

The Bible says:
Then the king sent to him a captain of fifty with his fifty men. So he went up to him; and there he was, sitting on the top of a hill. And he spoke to him:

Consuming Fire for Fire

"Man of God, the king has said, come down!" So Elijah answered and said to the captain of fifty, 'If I am a man of God, then let fire come down from heaven and consume you and your fifty men." And fire came down from heaven and consumed him and his fifty. Then he sent him another captain of fifty with his fifty men. And he answered and said to him, "man of God thus has the king said, 'Come down quickly!'" So Elijah answered and said to them, "If I am a man of God, let fire come down from heaven and consume you and your fifty men." And the fire of God came down from heaven and consumed him and his fifty. - (2 Kings 1:9-12)

You can also pray similar prayers in faith and get similar results. The Bible says Elijah was a man with like passions like us.

PRAYERS:

1. *In the Mighty name of Jesus Christ, I command the all-consuming fire of God to burn into ashes any thing in my life, which is not of God. Let them catch fire and burn into ashes in Jesus name.*

2. *In the Mighty name of Jesus Christ, I command the all-consuming fire of God to burn up into*

ashes every witchcraft contamination through food, water and sex in my life in Jesus name.

3. I command the consuming fire of the Holy Ghost to burn up into ashes every satanic, witchcraft, and demonic deposit inside of my body in Jesus name. I command them to come out of my body now in Jesus name.

4. I command the all-consuming fire of God to burn into ashes every satanic, witchcraft and demonic sicknesses deposited in my body. I command them to burn up and come out of me now in Jesus name.

5. In the Mighty name of Jesus Christ, I command the all-consuming fire of the Holy Spirit to burn into ashes every witchcraft curses operating against me and my family in Jesus name.

6. In the Mighty name of Jesus Christ, I command the fire of God to burn into ashes every spirit of weakness, tiredness, fatigue, hopelessness, and discouragement holding me captive in Jesus name.

7. In the Mighty name of Jesus Christ, I command the all-consuming fire of the Holy Spirit to burn

into ashes every body pains I am experiencing now in Jesus name.

8. I command the fire of God to break me loose and free from every witchcraft and demonic slavery in Jesus name.

9. I command the fire of God to deliver me from mental confusion in Jesus name.

10. I command the fire of God to burn into ashes every generational stronghold keeping me bound in Jesus name.

11. I command the fire of God to burn into ashes every spirit blocking me from getting a job in Jesus name. I consume into ashes the spirit of jobless and unemployment in my life in Jesus name.

12. I command the all-consuming fire to burn into ashes every marital conflict in Jesus name.

13. I command the all-consuming fire of God to burn into ashes every witches operating against me in the church, house, and work place in Jesus name.

14. *In the Mighty name of Jesus Christ, I command the consuming fire of God to burn into ashes every spirit of defeat, failure, non-achievement, unfruitfulness, and unproductiveness that is operating against me through witchcraft. I command them to burn into ashes in Jesus name. I am fruitful and productive in Jesus name.*

15. *In the Mighty name of Jesus Christ, I command the consuming fire of God to burn into ashes every witchcraft attack against my body through sicknesses and diseases in Jesus name. I receive my healing right now in Jesus name.*

16. *In the Mighty name of Jesus Christ, If I be a child of God, I command the all-consuming fire of God to burn into ashes every witchcraft spells, curses, charm, hexes, voodoo and obeah that is working against me and my family.*

17. *I command the all-consuming fire of God to burn into ashes every bond of wickedness afflicting my life now in Jesus name.*

18. *I command the all-consuming fire of God to burn into ashes every yoke of oppressing holding me in bondage in Jesus name.*

19. In the Mighty name of Jesus Christ, I command the all-consuming fire of the Holy Ghost to burn into ashes every satanic plans, plot, schemes, conspiracy, projection, expectation, devices and imaginations against me and my family in Jesus name. I command you to catch fire and be destroyed in Jesus name.

20. I command the consuming fire of God to burn into ashes the spirit of fear, anxiety, panic, worry, stress and nervousness in Jesus name. I command you to catch fire and die in my life in Jesus name. I receive the spirit of joy, love, peace, and sound mind in the Mighty name of Jesus

21. I command the consuming fire of God to burn into ashes every demons of depression, suicidal thoughts, and spirit of heaviness oppressing me in Jesus name. I command you to catch fire and die in my life in Jesus name.

22. In the Mighty name of Jesus Christ, I command the all-consuming fire of the Holy Ghost to burn into ashes every witchcraft and demonic limitations, restriction, and imprisonment put upon my life in Jesus name. I break loose and free by fire and by force in Jesus name.

23. Let the all-consuming fire of God burn into ashes every demon and witchcraft spirits causing barrenness and miscarriages in my life in Jesus name.

24. Let the all-consuming fire of God burn into ashes every witchcraft and demonic strongman frustrating my life in Jesus name. I command you to catch fire and die in Jesus name.

25. I command the fire of God to burn into ashes every demon and witchcraft spirit attacking my finances and job in Jesus name. I command you to catch fire and die in Jesus name.

26. I command every evil altars speaking against my life and destiny to catch fire and burn into ashes in Jesus name.

27. I command every invisible walls and mountains blocking me from breaking through in life to catch fire and burn into ashes in Jesus name.

28. I command every satanic problems assigned against me in my work place to catch fire and burn into ashes in Jesus name.

29. In the Mighty name of Jesus Christ, I command the fire of God to burn into ashes every satanic

gate and doors shut before my dreams and visions in Jesus name.

30. I command the fire of God to burn into ashes every demon causing me to miss my opportunities in life in Jesus name.

31. Let the consuming fire of God burn into ashes all witchcraft and demonic attacks causing financial hardship in my life in Jesus name.

32. In the Mighty name of Jesus Christ, I release the fire of God against the spirit of fear, stress, insomnia, tension, confusion, and restlessness in Jesus name.

CHAPTER 8

EXPOSED BY THE FIRE OF GOD

> *But When Paul had gathered a bundle of sticks and laid them on the fire, a viper came out because of the heat, and fastened on his hand. So when the natives saw the creature hanging from his hand, they said to one another, " No doubt this man is a murderer, whom, though he has escaped the sea, yet justice does not allow to live." But he shook off the creature into the fire and suffered no harm. However, they were expecting that he would swell up or suddenly fall down dead. But after they had looked for a long time and saw no harm come to him, they changed their minds and said that he was a god. -(Act 28 vs. 3 to 6)*

The fire of God separates the genuine from the fake. It separates the good from the bad, spiritual from the carnal, and also pure from the impure. On the day of Pentecost, the tongues of fire distinguished the Christians from the unbelievers. When Shadrach, Meshach, and Abed-Nego were put into the fiery burning furnace, they survived the fire and did not die but the fire consumed the people who put them into the fire.

Therefore, because the king's command was urgent, and the furnace exceedingly hot, the flame of the fire killed those men who took up Shadrach, Meshach, and Abed-Nego. -(Daniel 3 vs. 22)

> *And these three men, Shadrach, Meshach, and Abed-Nego, fell down bound into the midst of the burning fiery furnace. Then King Nebuchadnezzar was astonished; and he rose in haste and spoke, saying to his counselors, " Did we not cast three men bound into the midst of the fire?" They answered and said to the King, " True, O king." "Look!" he answered, " I see four men loose, walking in the midst of the fire; and they are not hurt, and the form of the fourth is like the Son of God."-(Daniel 3 vs. 23 to 25)*

The fire of God through prayers has the ability to expose the hidden things of darkness into the broad daylight. From the scripture from the book of Act we discover that the viper was comfortably hiding in the midst of the wood without any body detecting it. The only time it was exposed is when it came into contact with the fire. The heat of the fire was unbearable for it so it came out in a hurry to escape. But Paul shook it back into the fire to be killed.

Today, we have human vipers or snakes who disguise themselves as friends, best friends, co-workers, and family relations yet they are snakes hidden under grass. You can never tell the true nature of these vipers until you smoke them out of their hiding place with the heat of fiery prayers.

But when he (John) saw many of the Pharisees and Sadducees coming to his baptism, he said to them, Brood of vipers! Who warned you to flee from the wrath to come? - (Matthew 3 vs. 7)

Jesus said to the Pharisee:

> *Brood of vipers! How can you, being evil, speak good things? For out of the abundance of the heart the mouth speaks. -(Matthew 12 vs. 34)*

CHARACTERISTICS OF VIPERS:

- Their assignment is to befriend you in the physical realm and monitor your destiny.
- Their assignment is to block you from manifesting your full potential in life.

- They gather relevant information from you in the physical realm and use it against you in the spiritual realm.
- They can be in your life for a long time undetected and cause a lot of havoc to your destiny.
- They become angry with you when you start praying the Holy Ghost fire prayers.
- They will even try to discourage you from praying the Holy Ghost fire prayers.
- They gradually distance themselves from you because of the heat of the fire prayers.
- Their assignment is to cause you to win their trust and share your plans with them so that they can sabotage it from manifesting in the physical realm in your life.
- They are satanic spies and agents working against God's purposes in your life.
- They can claim to be your best friend yet spiritually be responsible for all your problems.
- They can be your close relations or relatives yet practicing witchcraft against you in the midnight.
- They can disguise themselves to like you but hate you behind your back.
- They can be the nicest people around you, you may pray, fellowship, eat, and go out with them and yet they practice witchcraft against you in their coven.

- They have the Judas spirit and will betray you to the devil to steal your glory.
- They have the spirit of Achan and will cause you to be defeated in life.

The only sure way to deal with this unfriendly friends and satanic vipers is to pray them out of your life. As long as you make them comfortable in your life, they will use their witchcraft to destroy you and limit your destiny on this earth.

It is about time you release the hot fire of God to expose and destroy the works of satanic vipers in your life in Jesus name. Remember, when you start doing aggressive prayers with the fire of God, you will notice that some people in your life will feel uncomfortable around you. They will begin to distance themselves from you. You will lose some so-called friends. They will walk out of your life without a reason. They true reason is that the heat of your fiery prayers is disturbing their witchcraft activities against you in the spiritual realm.

PRAYER TOPICS: (EXPOSE BY FIRE)

1. In the Mighty name of Jesus Christ, I command the all-consuming fire of God to expose every witch in my life in Jesus name.

Consuming Fire for Fire

2. In the Mighty name of Jesus Christ, I command the judgment fire of God to expose every witch or wizard who has disguised them selves as friends or relatives in Jesus name.

3. Let the fire of God expose very vipers in my life in Jesus name.

4. Let the unquenchable fire of God expose and burn every external enemy in my life in Jesus name.

5. Whatever my enemies have used to cover up their faces from being seen by me let it be exposed by fire in Jesus name.

6. I command the fire of God to burn up and expose every snake agents around me in Jesus name. Let all the snakes in my life be exposed from today in Jesus name.

7. Every snake agent responsible for my problems, be exposed by the consuming fire of God in Jesus name.

8. Let the judgment fire of God burn and expose all satanic vipers in my family, marriage, work place and church in Jesus name.

9. *I command all witches and wizard around me to be exposed by fire in Jesus name.*

10. *I command the fire of God to torment all the witches and wizards fighting against me and expose them all in Jesus name.*

11. *Every witch fighting against my destiny be exposed by fire in Jesus name. Be tormented by the unquenchable fire of God in Jesus name.*

12. *Every witch afflicting my body with sickness and diseases be exposed by fire in Jesus name. Let the fire of God torment you in Jesus name.*

13. *Every witch fighting me at my place of work be exposed by fire in Jesus name. Let the sulfur fire of God torment you in Jesus name.*

14. *Every witch troubling my marriage be exposed by fire in Jesus name. Let the wind of fire torment you in Jesus name.*

15. *Every witch troubling my spouse and children be exposed by fire in Jesus name. Let the fire of God torment you in Jesus name.*

16. Every satanic agent responsible for my down fall in life, be exposed by fire in Jesus name. Let the fire of God torment you in Jesus name.

17. Every satanic spy in my life, monitoring my life and destiny be exposed by fire in Jesus name. Let the fire of God torment you in Jesus name.

18. I command every Judas and Achan in my life to be exposed by fire in Jesus name. Let the fire of God torment them from their hiding place.

19. God arise and expose all my enemies by fire in Jesus name.

PRAYER TOPICS: (DISARM BY FIRE)

1. In the Mighty name of Jesus Christ, I disarm my enemies of all their weapons being used against me in Jesus name.

2. **Let the fire of God burn into ashes every weapon released against me in judgment in Jesus name.**

3. I command the all-consuming fire to burn into ashes every weapon of witchcraft, black magic, sorcery, voodoo, obeah, curses and hexes being used against me and my family in Jesus name.

4. Let the judgment fire of God disarm my enemies of their entire weapon today in Jesus name.

5. Let the evil weapons of my enemies catch fire now and burn into ashes in Jesus name.

6. I render by enemies impotent by fire of God in Jesus name.

7. I disarm all my enemies by fire in Jesus name.

8. I render my enemies weaponless by fire in Jesus name.

9. I render my enemies powerless by fire in Jesus name.

10. I render all the weapons of my enemies useless and void in Jesus name.

11. From today, I declare by the fire of God that no weapon of my enemies formed against me and my family shall prosper in my life in Jesus name.

PRAYER TOPICS (DISGRACE BY FIRE)

1. God arise and disgrace all my enemies who have surrounded me by fire in Jesus name.

2. God arise and humiliate my enemies before my very face by fire in Jesus name

3. God arise and embarrass all my enemies by fire in Jesus name.

4. Let my enemies fall into every pit they have dug for me by fire in Jesus name.

5. Let my enemies be ensnared by the traps they have set for me by fire in Jesus name.

6. Let every evil arrow shot against me backfire in Jesus name. Let it return back to sender in Jesus name.

7. Let every curse spoken against me backfire in Jesus name. Let it return back to sender in Jesus name.

8. Let every witchcraft, hexes, charm, voodoo, and obeah done against me backfire in Jesus name. Let it go back to the sender in Jesus name.

9. Let all my enemies be confused and disgrace before me now in Jesus name.

10. God arise, and don't let the evil expectations and imagination of my enemies come to pass in my life in Jesus name.

11. God arise and fight for me in Jesus name. Let anyone destroying my reputation be disgraced by fire in Jesus name.

12. Let anyone destroying my marriage and family be disgraced by fire in Jesus name.

13. Let anyone who is attacking my destiny and glory be disgraced in Jesus name.

14. Let anyone who is destroying my finances, business, and job be disgraced in Jesus name.

15. Let anyone who is destroying my health with sickness and diseases be disgraced in Jesus name.

16. Let anyone who is wishing my downfall be disgraced in Jesus name.

17. Let anyone who is practicing witchcraft on me be disgraced in Jesus name.

18. Let anyone who is plotting, devising, planning, and conspiring evil against me and my family be disgraced in Jesus name.

19. In the Mighty name of Jesus Christ, Let anyone who is behind by problems in life be disgraced in Jesus name.

PRAYER TOPICS: (DESTROY BY FIRE)

1. In the Mighty name of Jesus Christ, I destroy by fire every witchcraft and demonic weapons formed against me and my family in Jesus name.

2. I destroy by fire every witchcraft hexes and spell released against me and my family in Jesus name.

3. I destroy by fire every sickness released against me in Jesus name.

4. I destroy by fire every evil plan of my enemies against me in Jesus name.

5. I destroy by fire the arrow of sorrow and disaster released against me in Jesus name.

6. *I destroy by fire the arrow of disappointment released against me in Jesus name. Let fire burn it in Jesus name.*

7. *I destroy by fire the arrow of rejection released against me in Jesus name. Let fire burn it in Jesus name.*

8. *In the Mighty name of Jesus, I destroy by the fire of God every evil implantation in my body let it burn into ashes in Jesus name.*

9. *I destroy by fire every evil implantation in my marriage in Jesus name. Let fire burn it in Jesus name.*

10. *I destroy by fire witchcraft arrows shot against me in Jesus name. Let fire burn it in Jesus name.*

PRAYER TOPICS: (SHAKE INTO FIRE):

1. *In the Mighty name of Jesus Christ, I shake into the consuming fire a viper or agent of darkness hanging around my life to destroy me. Let fire burn you in Jesus name*

2. **In the Mighty name of Jesus Christ, I shake into fire a snake agent monitoring my life in Jesus name. Let fire burn you in Jesus name.**

3. I shake every witch practicing witchcraft on me into fire in Jesus name. Let the consume fire burn you in Jesus name.

4. **I shake every agent of darkness assigned to mislead and destroy me into the fire of God. Let fire burn you in Jesus name.**

5. In the Mighty name of Jesus Christ, I shake every evil eye manipulating my destiny into the fire of God in Jesus name. Let the fire of God burn you today in Jesus name.

6. **I shake every serpentine demon that has coiled itself around my life into the fire of God. In Jesus name, let the fire consume you.**

7. In the Mighty name of Jesus Christ, I shake into the fire of God every python demon, which has coiled itself around me to squeezed life out of me. I command the fire of God to burn you into ashes in Jesus name.

8. *Every cloth of shame and reproach that has been put on me by witches, I shake it off my body into the fire of God in Jesus name.*

9. *All witchcraft spells and charms operating against me. I shake them off my life and cast them into the consuming fire of God in Jesus name.*

10. Every demonic yoke operating against me, today I shake the yoke off my life and cast it into the fire of God to be consumed in Jesus name.

11. **I shake off the spirit of poverty into fire in Jesus name. Let fire burn you in Jesus name.**

12. I shake off the spirit of rejection, disfavor and disappointment into the fire of God in Jesus name. Let fire burn them all in Jesus name.

13. I shake off from my life, the spirit of failure and defeat. Let fire burn them all in Jesus name.

14. **In the Mighty name of Jesus Christ, I shake off from my life the spirit of delay, stagnation and retrogression. Let fire consume you all into ashes in Jesus name.**

CHAPTER 9

FIRE 4 FIRE PRAYERS

And these three men, Shadrach, Meshach, and Abed-Nego, fell down bound into the midst of the burning fiery furnace. Then King Nebuchadnezzar was astonished; and he rose in haste and spoke, saying to his counselors, " Did we not cast three men into the midst of the fire?" They answered and said to the king, " True, O king." Look! he answered, "I see four men loose, walking in the midst of the fire; and they were not hurt, and the form of the fourth is like the Son of God.-(Daniel 3 vs. 23 to 25)

We have Satanic fire or problems which are orchestrated and designed by the devil and his agents to destroy the Child of God; however, if you put your whole trust in the Lord Jesus Christ, He will always be there to deliver you from all evil. Satanic fiery problems will not be able to consume and destroy you once your faith in God is steadfast. Whatever situation you are going through, simply put your trust in the

Lord Jesus Christ and He will deliver you from the problem.

> *Trust in the LORD with all your heart, and lean not on your own understanding. In all your ways acknowledge Him, And He Shall direct your paths. -(Proverbs 3 vs. 5 to 6)*

> *Many are the afflictions of the righteous, but the LORD delivers him out of them all. He guards all his bones; not one of them is broken. Evil shall slay the wicked, and those who hate the righteous shall be condemned. -(Psalm 34 vs.19 to 21)*

Cast your burden on the LORD, and He shall sustain you; He shall never permit the righteous to be moved. -(Psalm 55 vs. 22)

When you totally put your faith and confidence in God, He will fight for you and also send forth His angel to rescue you from every satanic fiery problem. There is an angel of the Lord who has power over fire; he will come through for you when you call upon the name of the Lord Jesus.

And another angel came out from the altar, who had power over fire. -(Revelation 14 vs. 18)

> *When you pass through the waters, I will be with you; And through the rivers, they shall not overflow you. When you walk through the fire, you shall not be burned, nor shall the flame scorch you. -(Isaiah 43 vs. 2)*

In the Mighty name of Jesus Christ, I command every satanic fiery problems released into your life to consume and destroy you to be quenched by the Holy Ghost in Jesus name. Let the angel of God rescue you from every demonic and witchcraft fiery problems in Jesus name. You shall not be burned by satanic fire in Jesus name. And the flames of the fire shall not scorch you either in Jesus Mighty name. Receive your deliverance now in Jesus Mighty name.

WITH THIS ENCOURAGEMENT, GET READY TO DO SOME SERIOUS FIRE 4 FIRE WARFARE PRAYERS IN JESUS NAME. YOU ARE MORE THAN A CONQUERER IN JESUS NAME.

But thus you shall deal with them: you shall destroy their altars and break down their sacred pillars, and cut down their wooden images, and burn their carved images with fire. -(Deuteronomy 7 vs. 5)

> *But the LORD your God will deliver them over to you, and will inflict defeat upon them until*

they are destroyed. And He will deliver their kings into your hand, and you will destroy their name from under the heaven; no one shall be able to stand against you until you have destroyed them. You shall burn the carved images of their gods with fire. -(Deuteronomy 7 vs. 23 to 25)

Therefore understand today that the LORD your God is He who goes over before you as a consuming fire. He will destroy them and bring them down before you; so you shall drive them out and destroy them quickly, as the LORD has said to you. -(Deuteronomy 9 vs. 3)

And I will give power to my two witnesses, and they will prophesy one thousand two hundred and sixty days, clothed in sackcloth. These are the two olive trees and the two lampstands standing before the God of the earth. And if anyone wants to harm them, fire proceeds out from their mouth and devours their enemies. And if anyone wants to harm them, he must be killed in this manner. -(Revelation 11 vs. 3 to 5)

PRAYERS AGAINST STAR HUNTERS:

1. In the Mighty name of Jesus Christ, Let the consuming fire of God burn into ashes anyone destroying my glory and destiny in Jesus name.

2. **Let the consuming fire of God burn into ashes any strongman/strongwoman who is sitting on my glory in Jesus name.**

3. Let the judgment fire of God burn into ashes anyone who is after my star and glory in Jesus name. Let fire burn you in Jesus name.

4. **I command the fire of God to burn every star hunter in my life in Jesus name.**

5. Anyone who has buried by glory and destiny let fire burn you in Jesus name.

6. **Any witch or wizard who is frustrating my destiny let fire burn you in Jesus name.**

7. Any strongman/strongwoman who has turned my glory and destiny upside down, Let the consuming fire of God burn you in Jesus name.

8. **Any agent of darkness that is frustrating my star, glory and destiny in life, I command the consuming fire of God to burn you in Jesus name.**

9. Any witch who has repackaged my star, glory and destiny, I command the unquenchable fire of God to burn you in Jesus name.

10. Any strongman who is manipulating my star and glory to fail let fire burn you now in Jesus name.

11. **Any demon or agent of darkness who is blocking my star from shining, catch fire and die in Jesus name.**

12. Any agent of darkness who has switched my glory and honor with someone else, I command the all-consuming fire of God to burn you in Jesus name.

13. **I command every star hunter who has resolved not to see me prosper to die by fire in Jesus name.**

14. I command every strongman/strongwoman who has vowed not to see me succeed in life to die by fire in Jesus name.

15. **I command every agent of darkness who has resolved to destroy me to die by fire in Jesus name.**

16. Any one who is messing around with my destiny, dreams, vision and aspirations in life, I command the consuming fire of God to burn you into ashes in Jesus name.

17. **I command my star to appear in my life by fire by force in Jesus name.**

18. Any one who wants to steal my glory, star and purpose, let fire burn you in Jesus name.

19. **In the Mighty name of Jesus Christ, Let fire burn anyone who is trying to destroy my star, glory and purpose in life in Jesus name.**

20. In the Mighty name of Jesus Christ, I command the fire of God to burn any one who is trying to kill my star and glory from shining in Jesus name.

21. **Anyone who is trying to kill me, let fire burn you in Jesus name.**

22. I command total restoration of my stolen glory, star, and virtues by fire by force in Jesus name.

23. **In the Mighty name of Jesus Christ, I command my destiny, glory and star to be retrieved by fire and by force from the camp of my enemies in Jesus name.**

24. I command my destiny to begin to manifest by fire and by force from today in Jesus name.

25. I command my star and glory to shine by fire and by force from today in Jesus name.

26. I command my dreams, vision and purpose to begin to manifest this year by fire and by force in Jesus name.

PRAYERS AGAINST MARINE DEMONS:

1. *In the Mighty name of Jesus Christ, I command the all-consuming fire of God to burn down the meeting place of the marine kingdom against me in Jesus name.*

2. *In the Mighty name of Jesus Christ, I command hailstones and fire to burn down the covens of the marine kingdom against me in Jesus name.*

3. *Any agent who mention my name in the marine kingdom let fire and lightning strike them and burn them in Jesus name.*

4. *I declare war by the fire of God against you spirit husband and wife in Jesus name.*

5. *Every spirit husband/wife that attacks me in my sleep, I command the fire of God to burn you into ashes in Jesus name.*

6. *Every spirit husband/wife that attacks me in my dream, let fire burn you in Jesus name.*

7. *Every blood covenant I have with you spirit husband and wife let it be consumed by the fire of God in Jesus name.*

8. *Every wedding and engagement ring put on my fingers by the spiritual spouse, let it be consumed by fire and removed from my hands by fire in Jesus name.*

9. *Every wedding gown and dress given to me by the spiritual spouse let it be consumed into ashes in Jesus name.*

10. *I command the all-consuming fire to burn into ashes every spirit husband/wife that comes to have sex with me in my dreams in Jesus name.*

11. *I command the fire of God to consume into ashes every spiritual babies produce as a result of intercourse with spirit husband.*

12. *I command every stronghold of the spirit husband/wife in my life to be consumed by fire in Jesus name.*

13. I torment you spirit husband/wife against me by the fire of God.

14. I release hail and fire against you spirit wife or husband in Jesus name. I resist you today in Jesus name.

15. I release live coals of fire against you spirit husband/wife in Jesus name. I resist you today in Jesus name.

16. I release the burning wind of God to burn up you spirit husband/wife in Jesus name. I rebuke you in Jesus mighty name.

17. I command the sulfur fire of God to consume you spirit husband and wife. I break myself free from your bondage and captivity in Jesus name.

18. Any time you spirit husband/wife try to have sex with me or sexually harass me let the fire of God burn you in Jesus name.

19. Any spiritual spouse that tries to attack me in my sleep let fire consume you in Jesus name.

20. Any spirit husband/wife that tries to appear in my dream to harass me, let the fire of God consume you in Jesus name.

21. Any marine demon that tries to come close to me, let the fire of God consume you in Jesus name.

22. Any point of contact in my body by marine spirit, catch fire and be destroyed in Jesus name.

23. Any marine deposit inside of my body, catch fire and be destroyed in Jesus name. I command you to come out of my body now in Jesus name.

24. Any marine serpent inside of me or attacking me from outside, die by fire in Jesus name.

25. Every serpentine spirit from the marine kingdom assigned against me, die by fire in Jesus name.

26. Every marine agents, assigned against me to destroy me, die by fire in Jesus name.

27. I command family marine household witchcraft operating against me to be scattered by fire in Jesus name.

28. Any marine priest or priestess working against me, die by fire in Jesus name.

29. I electrify my whole body with the consuming fire of God in Jesus name.

30. Any marine demons that try to trespass to touch me let the fire of God burn you up in Jesus name.

31. I command the horses and chariots of fire of God to protect me in my dream world in Jesus name.

32. I command the horses and chariots of fire of God to protect me from marine attacks when I am asleep in Jesus name.

33. I command the horses and chariot of fire of God to protect me from all marine activities in Jesus name.

34. God arise today, and scatter every marine spirits assigned against me in Jesus name.

35. I receive my deliverance my fire and by force from every marine husband and wife in Jesus name.

36. I declare and decree my deliverance by fire and by force in Jesus name.

PRAYERS AGAINST DEMONIC ATTACKS:

1. In Jesus Mighty name, I command every demonic spirits troubling me to catch fire and die in Jesus name.

2. I command every demonic activity in my life to be consumed by the fire of God in Jesus name.

3. Let the fire of God destroy every demonic activity in my marriage in Jesus name.

4. Let the fire of God destroy all demonic activities in my children's lives in Jesus name.

5. Let the fire of God destroy all demonic activities in my husband/wife lives in Jesus name.

6. Let the fire of God consume every demonic activity in my body in Jesus name.

7. Let the fire of God consume all demonic activities in my house, apartment and workplace in Jesus name.

8. Let the fire of God consume every demonic spirit afflicting my body with pain in Jesus name.

9. Let the fire of God consume every demonic spirit hindering me in life in Jesus name.

10. I command the fire of God to burn up every demonic spirit frustrating my life in Jesus name.

11. I command every internal demon to catch fire and die in Jesus name.

12. I command the fire of God to burn up every demon given the assignment to kill, steal and destroy me. Let them catch fire and die in Jesus name.

13. I command every blood-sucking demon after my life to catch fire and die in Jesus name.

14. Let the fire of God; consume every demon wasting my life in Jesus name. Let them catch fire and die in Jesus name.

15. I command the fire of God to consume every demonic marks, tag, and label placed upon my life for destruction. Let the fire of God burn them up in Jesus name.

16. *I command the fire of God to destroy every demonic harassment and intimidation in my life in Jesus name.*

17. *Let the fire of God consume into ashes every demonic sickness and infirmities planted in my body. Let fire burn the demons in Jesus name.*

18. *I command the all-consuming fire of God to burn into ashes every demonic attacks and calculations designed to hinder me from fulfilling my destiny this year. Let the fire of God burn the demons in Jesus name.*

19. *I command the fire of God to burn every demonic bondage that I have been put in, in Jesus name.*

20. *Demonic cage in my life, burn by fire in Jesus name.*

21. *Demonic chains and shackles in my life burn by the fire of God in Jesus name.*

22. *Demonic yoke operating against me, burn by fire in Jesus name.*

23. *Demonic obstacles to my miracles burn by fire in Jesus name.*

24. Demonic marks and labels on me burn by fire in Jesus name.

25. Demonic curse and witchcraft against me burn by fire in Jesus name.

26. Demonic strongholds in my life burn by fire in Jesus name.

27. I release myself from all demonic slavery, bondage, and captivity by fire and by force in Jesus name. Let the fire of God burn every demon troubling me in Jesus name.

PRAYERS AGAINST WITCHCRAFT SPIRIT:

1. In the Mighty name of Jesus Christ, I command the fire of God to consume into ashes every witchcraft assignment against me in Jesus name.

2. I command the fire of God to burn into ashes every witchcraft curse, charm, spells, and hexes operating against me and my family in Jesus name.

3. I command the all-consuming fire of God to burn into ashes every witchcraft manipulation

and control over my life in Jesus name. Let it burn by fire in Jesus name.

4. Let the unquenchable fire of God consume into ashes every witchcraft intimidation and domineering over my life in Jesus name. Let it burn by fire in Jesus name.

5. I command every witchcraft weapons being used against me to catch fire and be destroyed in Jesus name.

6. I command every witchcraft pot, crystal ball, monitoring mirror and monitoring device to catch fire now and burn into ashes in Jesus name.

7. Every witchcraft attack on my body catch fire now and be destroyed in Jesus name.

8. Every witchcraft attack on my job, business, and education catch fire now and be destroyed.

9. Every witchcraft projection in my house and apartment, catch fire now and be destroyed in Jesus name.

10. Every witchcraft attacks in my sleep and dreams, catch fire now and be destroyed.

11. Every witchcraft attacks on my destiny, dreams, vision, and prophetic mandate in life this year, catch fire now and be destroyed in Jesus name.

12. Every witch affliction and torment in my life, catch fire now and be destroyed in Jesus name.

13. Every witchcraft attack in my family, catch fire now and be destroyed.

14. Every witchcraft attack on my children and spouse, catch fire now and be destroyed in Jesus name.

15. Every witchcraft attack on my finances and prosperity, catch fire now and be destroyed in Jesus name.

16. I command every witchcraft arrow against me and my family to backfire in Jesus name.

17. I command every witchcraft attack against my health to backfire now in Jesus name.

18. I command every witchcraft darts and stones released against me to backfire now in Jesus name.

19. I command the all-consuming fire of God to burn into ashes every witchcraft assignment, plots, devices, plans, schemes, operations, and conspiracies taken against me in Jesus name.

20. I command every witchcraft spirit troubling me to die by the fire of God in Jesus name.

21. I command every witchcraft agent attacking me to catch fire and perish in Jesus name.

22. Let the fire of God consume every witchcraft attack affecting my mind in Jesus name.

23. Let the fire of God consume every witchcraft attack affecting my emotions in Jesus name.

24. Let the fire of God consume every witchcraft attack influencing my actions in Jesus name.

25. Let the fire of God consume into ashes every witchcraft that is controlling my decision and will in Jesus name.

26. I command every witchcraft network operating against me to be destroyed by fire now in Jesus name.

27. I command every witchcraft agenda and calendar against me to be consumed into ashes by the fire of God in Jesus name.

28. Let fire burn every witch who releases a curse against me in Jesus name.

29. Let fire burn down into ashes the coven of the witches who meet against me in Jesus name.

30. Let fire burn any witch who rises against me and my family. Let them perish by fire in Jesus name.

31. Any harm that has been done to me and my family by witches let it be destroyed today by the fire of God in Jesus name.

32. Let fire burn every witch in my life that pretends to be my friend in Jesus name.

33. Let fire burn every witch in my life that pretends to be my relative in Jesus name.

34. Let fire burn up every witch or wizard who tries to attack me in Jesus name.

35. Let the fire of God burn up every witch who tries to attack my marriage, family, children, spouse, and my properties in Jesus name.

36. Let fire burn into ashes every witchcraft powers attacking my life in Jesus name.

37. Let fire burn into ashes every witchcraft powers that is fighting against my finances in Jesus name.

38. Let fire burn into ashes every witchcraft powers that is working against my progress in life in Jesus name. Let fire burn them today in Jesus name.

39. Let fire burn into ashes every witchcraft contamination and pollution in my body through food and water in Jesus name.

40. In the Mighty name of Jesus Christ, I command the fire of God to consume and utterly destroy every witchcraft arrows, bullets, spells, projections, predictions, fiery darts, and stones released against me and my family. Let the fire of God burn them all in Jesus name.

PRAYERS AGAINST THE SPIRIT OF DELAY AND SETBACK:

1. In the Mighty name of Jesus Christ, I command every spirit of delay, retrogression, lateness, stagnancy and postponing fighting against me to catch fire and be consumed into ashes in Jesus name.

2. Any spirit blocking me from getting a job catch fire and die in Jesus name.

3. Any spirit blocking me from getting pregnant catch fire and die in Jesus name.

4. Any spirit blocking me from getting my breakthrough and miracle this year, catch fire and die in Jesus name.

5. Any demon and witchcraft spirit hindering me from making progress in life, catch fire and perish in Jesus name.

6. Any spirits delaying my destiny catch fire and perish in Jesus name.

7. Any demon and witchcraft spirit hindering me from getting married, I command the fire of God to consume you now in Jesus name. Die by fire in Jesus name.

8. *Any demon and witchcraft spirit that is blocking me from finishing my education, I command you to die by fire in Jesus name.*

9. *Any demonic spirit causing me to fail my exams, catch fire and die in Jesus name.*

10. *Any spirit of bad luck that follows me, I command you to die by fire in Jesus name.*

11. *Any spirit of disappointment that follows my life, catch fire and die in Jesus name.*

12. *Any demon of failure and defeat that follows me, catch fire and die in Jesus name.*

13. *You spirit of anti progress that follows me, I command you to die by fire in Jesus name.*

14. *You demon of rise and fall that follows me to destroy me, I command you to catch fire and die in Jesus name.*

15. *I command every obstacle to my miracle to be consumed by the fire of God in Jesus name.*

16. *I command the fire of God to consume every satanic embargo in my life in Jesus name.*

17. I command the all-consuming fire of God to burn into ashes every satanic roadblock hindering my destiny in Jesus name. Catch fire and burn into ashes in Jesus name.

18. Let the all-consuming fire of God burn into ashes every satanic barricade blocking me from succeeding in life in Jesus name. Catch fire and burn into ashes in Jesus name.

19. Let the fire of God burn down every satanic road traffic slowing me down in life in Jesus name.

20. Let the fire of God burn down into ashes every satanic load and weights slowing me down in life. Catch fire and burn into ashes in Jesus name.

21. I command every stumbling block to my destiny this year to clear from my path by the fire of God in Jesus name.

22. I command every invisible wall blocking me from moving forward in life, to catch fire and burn down into ashes in Jesus name.

23. I command every invisible mountain before me to melt by fire in Jesus name.

24. I command the fire of God to burn into ashes every demonic and witchcraft ropes binding me in life in Jesus name. Catch fire and burn into ashes in Jesus name.

25. I command every satanic chains and shackles holding me bound to break by fire now in Jesus name. Break by fire and by force in Jesus name.

26. I command every demonic and witchcraft cobweb holding me bound to catch fire and burn into ashes in Jesus name.

27. I command every demonic and witchcraft net holding me bound to catch fire and burn into ashes in Jesus name.

28. You spirit of delay die by fire in Jesus name.

PRAYER AGAINST PYTHON AND LEVIATHAN:

1. In the Mighty name of Jesus Christ, I use the sword of the spirit to cut off the head of every serpentine demon attacking me in Jesus name. I command you to catch fire and burn into ashes in Jesus name.

2. Every coiling serpent squeezing breath out of me, I use the sword of the spirit to cut you into pieces. I command you to die by the fire of God in Jesus name.

3. I break myself loose and free by fire and by force from every coiling serpentine demon in Jesus name.

4. I set live coals of fire into the belly of the python spirit to consume it in Jesus name. I command you to vomit me out of your belly by the fire of God and by force in Jesus name.

5. I rain sulfur fire on the head of the python spirit, I command you to uncoil yourself around me and loose me and let me go now in Jesus name.

6. I command the brimstone of fire to consume every python demon fighting against me in Jesus name. I command you to die by fire in Jesus name.

7. I release fire and sulfur to burn into ashes every python demon coiling itself around me to destroy me in Jesus name.

8. I release live coals of fire to consume into ashes every python spirit-choking destiny out of me in

Consuming Fire for Fire

Jesus name. I command you to die by fire in Jesus name.

9. I command the hot burning wind of God to burn up every python demon holding me captive in Jesus name.

10. I release hail and fire on the python demon who has taken me prisoner. Catch fire and die in Jesus name.

11. Let the all-consuming fire of God burn into ashes leviathan demon in Jesus name.

12. Let the hail and fire burn up the spirit of leviathan attacking me in Jesus name.

13. In the Mighty name of Jesus Christ, I release fire and sulfur against the spirit of leviathan holding me captive in Jesus name. Catch fire and die in Jesus name.

14. I release the hot burning wind of God to consume the spirit of leviathan troubling me in Jesus name.

15. I release myself by fire and by force from the stronghold of leviathan in Jesus name.

16. I command the stronghold of leviathan and python in my life to burn down into ashes in Jesus name.

17. I consume by fire the control and intimidation of python and leviathan over my life in Jesus name.

18. I break loose and free from the manipulation and influence of leviathan and python over my life in Jesus name.

19. Let the fire of God burn into ashes every leviathan demon stopping me from reading and meditating on the Bible in Jesus name. Catch fire and die in Jesus name.

20. Let fire burn into ashes every leviathan demon hindering me from praying and fasting. Catch fire and die in Jesus name.

21. Let fire burn into ashes every leviathan demon that causes me to sleep every time I am reading my Bible or Praying. Catch fire and die in Jesus name.

22. Let fire burn into ashes every leviathan demon and python demon that is causing me to be lukewarm Christian. Catch fire and die in Jesus name.

23. Let the fire of God burn into ashes every leviathan and python demon causing me to live in constant fear and depression. Catch fire and die in Jesus name.

24. Let fire burn every python and leviathan spirit that is chocking live, energy, strength, peace happiness, joy and sound mind out of me. Catch fire and die in Jesus name,

25. Let fire burn into ashes every python spirit that attacks me in my sleep and dreams. Catch fire and die in Jesus name.

26. Let fire consume every leviathan and python demon causing me to be weak, overwhelmed, and tired always. Catch fire and die in Jesus name.

27. I set the backbone of leviathan on fire. Let the all-consuming fire of God burn you up from my life in Jesus name.

28. I command the hot burning wind of God to burn up and drive python and leviathan spirit far from me in Jesus name.

29. I declare and decree my deliverance from python and leviathan demon by fire and by force in Jesus name. From today, the spirit of python and leviathan has no more power over me in Jesus name.

PRAYER AGAINST SATANIC AGENTS:

1. Any agent of darkness planted in my life to destroy me, scatter by fire in Jesus name.

2. **Let the fire of God scatter any messenger of Satan planted in my marriage to destroy it. Catch fire and perish in Jesus name.**

3. Let the fire of God scatter any agent of darkness planted at my work place to trouble and cause me to lose my job. Catch fire and perish in Jesus name.

4. **Let the fire of God scatter any satanic agent planted in my children's lives to destroy them. Let them catch fire and perish in Jesus name.**

5. Let the fire of God scatter any satanic agent planted in my family to destroy me. Let them catch fire and perish in Jesus name.

6. ***Let the fire of God scatter any satanic agent planted in my spouse life to destroy them and my marriage in Jesus name. Let them catch fire and perish in Jesus name.***

7. *Let the fire of God consume and destroy every jezebelic spirit operating in my life to destroy my marriage in Jesus name.*

8. ***Any agent planted at my church to destroy me, catch fire and perish in Jesus name.***

9. *Any agent planted in my house assigned to destroy me, catch fire and perish in Jesus name.*

10. ***I command the consuming fire of God to burn and destroy every satanic spy or secret agent send to destroy my life. Let the fire of God consume you in Jesus name.***

11. *I command the judgment fire of God to consume and destroy any thing in my life that exalts itself against the knowledge of God for my life. Be consumed by fire in Jesus name.*

12. ***Let the consuming fire burn and destroy anything inside of me that is not of God in Jesus name. Internal demons and witchcraft spirit catch fire and die in Jesus name.***

13. Let the fire of God consume and destroy anything around me, which is not of God in Jesus name. External demons and witchcraft spirit die by fire in Jesus name.

PRAYERS AGAINST MARITAL ATTACKS:

1. **I command the fire of God to scatter the plans of witchcraft to destroy my marriage in Jesus name.**

2. Let the fire of God consume into ashes every seed of argument, misunderstanding, hate, unforgiveness, lack of communication, quarrel, and disrespect planted in my marriage to destroy it.

3. **Let the fire of God burn down into ashes very invisible walls separating me from my spouse in Jesus name.**

4. Let the fire of God consume into ashes every evil mask covering my marital glory in Jesus name.

5. Let the fire of God consume every bad behavior that is meant to destroy my marriage in Jesus name.

6. **Let the fire of God consume every witchcraft activity that has turned my spouse against me in Jesus name. Catch fire and be destroyed now in Jesus name.**

7. Every evil tree the devil has planted in my marriage, die by fire in Jesus name.

8. **I command the fire of God to consume into ashes the spirit of separation and divorce from my marriage in Jesus name.**

9. Let the fire of God consume and destroy any charms and spells controlling my spouse against me in Jesus name.

10. **I release my spouse from every spells and charms by fire and by force in Jesus name.**

11. I command the all-consuming fire of God to burn into ashes every black magic being done to destroy my marriage in Jesus name.

12. **Let all-consuming fire of God burn into ashes every invisible barrier that has been erected to separate my husband and me in Jesus name.**

13. Let the fire of God consume and scatter every witch/wizard controlling and manipulating my

marriage in Jesus name. Let them perish by fire in Jesus name.

14. Every witchcraft and black magic operating against my marriage be destroyed by fire in Jesus name.

15. Let the fire of God consume every unclean spirit operating on assignment against my marriage in Jesus name.

16. Let the fire of God consume into ashes every demon and witchcraft spirit influencing my spouse to divorce or be separated from me. Catch fire and die in Jesus name.

17. Let the fire of God locate and consume any persons or demonic spirit working behind the scenes to destroy my marriage in Jesus name.

18. Every spells and charms controlling me to destroy my marriage break by fire now in Jesus name.

19. I command every witchcraft spirit controlling my spouse mind to destroy our marriage to catch fire and be destroyed in Jesus name.

20. Let the fire of God consume and destroy the spirit of lust, pornography, masturbation, and all sexual immorality controlling my spouse in Jesus name.

21. **I command the fire of God to consume and destroy the spirit of adultery controlling the life of my spouse in Jesus name.**

22. Every bad advice given to my spouse by friends and relatives let it be consumed by fire in Jesus name.

23. **Any one who has an ungodly soul-tie with my spouse let it be consumed and destroyed by the fire of God in Jesus name.**

24. I destroy by the fire of God every witchcraft spirit controlling and manipulating my spouse actions and behavior to destroy our marriage in Jesus name. Catch fire and burn into ashes in Jesus name.

25. **I release the hot burning wind of fire to drive out from my spouse life bad friends and relatives in Jesus name.**

26. *I release the hot sulfur fire to drive out from my spouse life every strange woman he is having affairs with in Jesus name.*

27. **Any agent of darkness responsible for my marital problems, catch fire and perish in Jesus name.**

28. *Every strange woman interfering with my marriage, let fire burn you and drive you out from my marriage in Jesus name.*

29. **I command the hot burning wind of God to keep the strange woman far away from my husband in Jesus name. If she ever comes close to him, let the fire of God burn her and keep her out in Jesus name.**

30. *Every witchcraft charms and spells that have been done to my husband to steal his mind and love from me. I command the all-consuming fire of God to burn them into ashes today in Jesus name.*

31. **Let the fire of God consume every soul-tie between my husband and the strange woman in Jesus name.**

32. I break my spouse loose and free by fire and by force from the spells and charms of the strange woman in Jesus name.

33. I command the all-consuming fire of God to destroy every witchcraft attacks from my in-laws and family members to destroy my marriage in Jesus name.

34. Every contamination planted in my spouse through food, water, drink, and sex let it be consumed by fire in Jesus name.

35. I release my spouse from the bondage of lust in Jesus name. Let the refiners fire purify him or her in Jesus name.

36. I break the yoke of masturbation, pornography, and alcoholism from my spouse in Jesus name.

37. Every spirit husband and wife fighting my marriage, I command you to die by the fire of God in Jesus name.

38. Every generational curse of divorce and separateion influencing my marriage be destroyed by the fire of God in Jesus name.

39. Every marital problem released to break my marriage, catch fire and be destroyed in Jesus name.

40. Let the fire of God burn and drive out every strange woman from my husband in Jesus name.

41. Let the love or lust my husband has for the strange woman be consumed by the fire of God in Jesus name.

42. Let the lust or love the strange woman has for my husband be consumed into ashes in Jesus name.

43. Let the spirit of confusion and constant arguments between my husband and I catch fire and be destroyed in Jesus name.

44. I release love, joy, understanding, forgiveness, and peace back into my marriage by fire by force in Jesus name.

45. Any strange woman or man assigned to destroy my family let fire burn you in Jesus name.

46. Let fire burn the strange woman or man when they come close to my spouse to have affairs in Jesus name.

47. Let the fire of God bring argument and misunderstanding between my spouse and the strange women in Jesus name.

48. Let the strange woman develop sudden hate and dislike for my spouse by fire and by thunder in Jesus name.

49. Anytime my husband meet with the strange woman in bed let fire burn them to stop in Jesus name.

50. Anytime my spouse comes close to the strange woman let fire separate them in Jesus name.

51. Any jezebel or Delilah woman assigned to snatch my husband, let fire burn you in Jesus name.

52. Let fire burn any husband snatcher or home wrecker after my spouse in Jesus name.

PRAYERS AGAINST BARRENNESS/MISCARRIAGE

1. Let the spirit of barrenness catch fire and die in my life in Jesus name.

2. *Let the spirit of miscarriage catch fire and die in my life and marriage in Jesus name.*

3. *Let the fire of God consume into ashes every altar of bareness and miscarriages, catch fire and be destroyed in Jesus name.*

4. *I command every demon and witchcraft spirit that is causing miscarriage and barrenness in my life to catch fire and die in Jesus name.*

5. *Every blood-sucking demon or witchcraft spirit eating up my children in the spirit realm, I command you to catch fire and die in Jesus name.*

6. *Any witch who has stolen my eggs preventing me from being pregnant, I command you to catch fire and die in Jesus name.*

7. *Any evil eye monitoring my pregnancy, I command you to be blinded by the fire of God in Jesus name.*

8. *I break myself loose and free from the yoke of miscarriage and barrenness in Jesus name.*

9. I cover by pregnancy with the precious blood of Jesus Christ, Let the fire of God protect my pregnancy from miscarriage in Jesus name.

10. I command my pregnancy to manifest by fire and by force this month in Jesus name.

11. I receive my babies by faith and by fire this year in Jesus name.

12. I am delivered from the curse of barrenness and miscarriage in Jesus name.

13. Let God arise and scatter all my enemies by fire and by thunder in Jesus name.

14. I command every curse of barrenness operating against me catch fire and be destroyed in Jesus name.

PRAYERS AGAINST EDUCATIONAL CHALLENGES:

1. In the Mighty name of Jesus Christ, I command any strongman/strongwoman blocking me from moving forward with my education to die by fire and thunder in Jesus name.

2. *Let the fire and thunder of God strike every demon and witch that causes me to constantly fail my exams in Jesus name.*

3. *Let the fire and thunder burn into ashes every witchcraft spirits manipulating and delaying me from finishing my courses in school in Jesus name.*

4. *Let the fire and thunder strike any demon and witchcraft spirit that causes me to forget what I study during exams in Jesus name.*

5. *Let the fire and thunder of God burn and destroy every spells and charms working against my education and my children's education in Jesus name.*

6. *I command the fire and thunder of God to strike any agent of darkness who has stolen the glory of my children from excelling in school in Jesus name.*

7. *Let fire and thunder consume every demon and witchcraft spirit causing my children to fall in Jesus name.*

8. *Any demon, witchcraft spirit, charms, and hexes that causes me to go blank during exams, be consumed by fire and thunder in Jesus name.*

9. **Any strongman/woman who has resolved not to allow me to finish my education, I command you this day to die by fire and thunder in Jesus name.**

10. *Any witchcraft spirit and demonic spirit that has resolved not to let me pass my exams to move on with my education, I command you to die by fire and thunder in Jesus name.*

11. **Every obstacles to my education, be consumed into ashes by the fire of God and by thunder in Jesus name.**

12. *Every curse that is operating against me to deny me from graduating from school let it be consumed by fire and thunder in Jesus name.*

13. *Any demon or witchcraft agent assigned against me to prevent me from graduation from school, I command you this day to die by fire and thunder in Jesus name.*

14. **Any demonic and witchcraft spirit given the mandate to block my children from finishing**

their education and graduating, I command you to die by fire and thunder in Jesus name.

15. Every spirit of delay, lateness, and setback prolonging my stay in school, die by fire and thunder in Jesus mighty name.

PRAYERS AGAINST SINGLENESS:

1. In the Mighty name of Jesus Christ, I command the judgment fire of God to consume every marital spell of singleness put upon my life in Jesus name.

2. **Let the judgment fire of God consume every strongman who is denying me assess to my marital glory. I command you to die by fire in Jesus name.**

3. Let the fire of God consume and destroy any demon that repels my spouse from me in Jesus name.

4. **Let every spiritual marriage be consumed by the fire of God in Jesus name.**

5. I command every spiritual spouse to burn into ashes by the fire of God in Jesus name.

6. **I command every spiritual marriage to be consumed by fire in Jesus name.**

7. Let the fire of God consume every curse of singleness place upon me in Jesus name.

8. **Let the fire of God burn into ashes every evil mask put on my face to repel my spouse from me. Catch fire and burn into ashes.**

9. Any strongman that has turned my marital glory upside down, die by fire in Jesus name.

10. **I command every curse of disappointment from men to be consumed by fire in Jesus name.**

11. I command the all-consuming fire to burn into ashes every jezebelic spirit destroying my marital opportunities in Jesus name.

12. **I command the fire of God to burn and destroy every witchcraft activities working to keep me from marrying in Jesus name.**

13. Let the fire of God burn up into ashes the yoke of singleness from my life in Jesus name.

PRAYERS AGAINST ALTARS:

1. *In the Mighty name of Jesus Christ, I command the fire of God to consume every covenant I have with any satanic altars in Jesus name.*

1. *In the Mighty name of Jesus Christ, I command the unquenchable fire of God to consume every evil altar I was dedicated or initiated to in Jesus name.*

2. *In the Mighty name of Jesus Christ, I command the fire of God to consume into ashes every altar in my father's household operating curses against me. Catch fire and burn into ashes in Jesus name.*

3. *In the Mighty name of Jesus Christ, I command the fire of God to consume into ashes every altar in my mother's household speaking curses against me. Catch fire and burn down into ashes in Jesus name.*

4. *In the Mighty name of Jesus Christ, I command the judgment fire of God to consume into ashes every altar and shrine from my spouse's father and mothers lineage that is speaking curse over them in Jesus name.*

5. *I release the consuming fire of God to burn and destroy every ancestral altar and shrine that is operating curses against me in Jesus name.*

6. *Let the fire of God burn down into ashes every altar of failure and defeat in my life in Jesus name.*

7. *Let the fire of God burn down into ashes every altar of rejection and disappointment following my life in Jesus name.*

8. *Let the fire of God burn down into ashes every altar of delay and lateness in my life in Jesus name.*

9. *Let the fire of God burn down into ashes every altar and shrine frustrating and harassing my life and destiny. Catch fire and be destroyed in Jesus name.*

10. *Let the fire of God burn down every altar of poverty operating in my life in Jesus name.*

11. *Let the fire of God burn down every altar of sickness and diseases destroying my health in Jesus name. Catch fire and be destroyed today in Jesus name.*

12. Let the fire of God burn down into ashes every altar that is keeping me single. Catch fire and be destroyed in Jesus name.

13. Let the fire of God burn down into ashes every altar operating against my marriage with separation and divorce. Catch fire and be destroyed in Jesus name.

14. Let the fire of God scatter every altar against my marital glory in Jesus name.

15. Let the all-consuming fire of God burn down into ashes every altar fighting against my finances and my job in Jesus name. Catch fire and be destroyed in Jesus name.

16. Let the fire of God consume into ashes every altar of bareness and miscarriages. Catch fire and be destroyed in Jesus name.

17. Altar of premature death after my life, catch fire and be destroyed in Jesus name.

18. Altar of witchcraft operating against my star and glory, catch fire and be destroyed in Jesus name.

19. Altar from my mothers' bloodline controlling and manipulating my destiny, catch fire and be destroyed now in Jesus name.

20. Altar from my father's bloodline controlling and manipulating my destiny, catch fire and be destroyed now in Jesus name.

21. Altar of limitations and restrictions in life operating against me, catch fire and burn down into ashes in Jesus name.

22. Altar of shame and disgrace operating against me, In the name of Jesus Christ, I command you to catch fire and burn into ashes.

23. Let the fire of god burn down evil altars and shrine that is denying me access into my promotion and breakthrough in Jesus name. Catch fire and be destroyed in Jesus name.

24. Altar against my spouse and children be scattered by the fire of God in Jesus name.

PRAYERS TO RECOVER YOUR STAR AND GLORY:

1. *In the Mighty name of Jesus Christ, I am breaking through by fire and by force every wall of resistance and opposition in my life.*

2. *I enter into the witchcraft and demonic coven, camp, high places, store house, gift store, super market, and banks, I take back by force and by fire what the devil and his agent have stolen from me in Jesus name.*

3. *I demand by fire and by force from the witches and wizards to return to me my stolen glory, star, blessing, prosperity and honor in Jesus name. Restore by force and by fire now in Jesus name.*

4. *I demand by fire and by force from the witches and wizard the total restoration and restitution of all by stolen inheritance and birthrights in Jesus name. Restore by fire and by force now in Jesus name.*

5. *Heavenly father, in the Mighty name of Jesus Christ, by the power of the Holy Spirit, I uproot from my life and family every evil tree planted in*

my life to destroy me. I command it to catch fire and burn into ashes in Jesus name.

6. **In the Mighty name of Jesus Christ, I capture the stronghold from the hand of my enemies. I recover all my stolen breakthroughs and miracles in Jesus name.**

7. Let God arise and let every stronghold fighting my marriage and marital glory fall in the name of Jesus.

8. **In the Mighty name of Jesus Christ, I command every stronghold established against my glory and destiny to fall like the walls of Jericho.**

9. I take by force and violence from the hands of my enemies my glory, star, blessing, breakthroughs, miracles, healing, deliverance and total restoration. I recover all my inheritance by fire and by force in the Mighty name of Jesus.

10. In the Mighty name of Jesus Christ, I recover my marriage, children, spouse, health, finances, destiny, glory, miracles, and breakthroughs from the hand of my enemies in Jesus name.

11. In the Mighty name of Jesus Christ, I am breaking through my enemy's defense system. I recover from them all my stolen blessings in Jesus name.

12. Let God arise and let every stronghold fighting my sons and daughter fall in Jesus name.

13. Let God arise and let every stronghold fighting my wife/husband fall in the name of Jesus.

14. In the Mighty name of Jesus Christ, I command the fire of God to consume into ashes every shrine holding my glory captive in Jesus Christ.

15. In the Mighty name of Jesus Christ, I command the consuming fire of God to burn into ashes every altar holding my destiny captives.

16. In the Mighty name of Jesus Christ, I command the fire of God to burn into ashes every tree that contains my placenta or umbilical chord in Jesus name.

17. In the Mighty name of Jesus Christ, I uproot every tree that my glory is buried in Jesus name. I set that tree on fire in the name of Jesus.

18. By the power of the Holy Ghost, I command my glory, destiny and star to be retrieved from every buried ground in Jesus name.

19. **By the power of the Holy Ghost, I command my star, destiny and glory to be retrieved from every witchcraft covens in the name of Jesus.**

20. By the power of the Holy Ghost, I command my star, destiny and glory to be retrieved from the marine kingdom in Jesus name.

21. **By the power of the Holy Ghost, I command my star, destiny and glory to be retrieved from the underground kingdom in Jesus name.**

22. By the power of the Holy Ghost, I command my star, destiny and glory to be retrieved from the camp of my enemies in Jesus name.

23. **By the power of the Holy Ghost, I command my star, destiny and glory to be retrieved from the household witchcraft in the name of Jesus.**

24. By the power of the Holy Ghost, I command my star, destiny and glory to be retrieved from ancestral spirit, familiar spirit, monitoring spirit and stool dwarf spirit in Jesus name.

25. *By the power of the Holy Ghost, I command my star, destiny and glory to be retrieved from the satanic witchcraft supermarket in the name of Jesus.*

26. *By the power in the name of Jesus Christ, I command my destiny, star and glory to be retrieved from the demonic invisible world*

27. *In the name of Jesus Christ, any agent of darkness who has scattered my blessing, I command my blessings to be restored in Jesus Mighty name.*

28. *In the Mighty name of Jesus Christ, any strongman/woman who has scattered my benefactors from assisting me in life, I command my helpers to show up in my life and bless me now in Jesus name.*

29. *I command every strongman/woman who scatters good things from me to die by fire in Jesus name.*

30. *Any ladder, elevator, steps, and escalator removed or destroy to prevent me from moving up. I command it to be restored to take me higher in life in Jesus name.*

31. I command my divine bridge to be restored by fire and by force in Jesus name.

32. **I command by divine ladder, escalator, stair case, and elevator to be restored by fire and by force in Jesus name.**

33. In the Mighty name of Jesus Christ, I recover all my stolen glory, honor, virtue, blessing, favor, miracles, and breakthrough from the ancestral and familiar strongman in the name of Jesus.

34. **In the name of Jesus Christ, I recover my marriage, family, children, education, business, job, finances, prosperity, and destiny from the ancestral and familiar strongman in Jesus name.**

35. In the Mighty name of Jesus Christ, I command every blessing I have lost to the ancestral and familiar strongman to return to me now by fire and by force in the name of Jesus.

36. **I command my marriage to be recovered by fire by force in the name of Jesus.**

37. I command my business and job to be recovered by fire by force in Jesus name.

38. *I command my education to be recovered by fire by force in Jesus name.*

39. *I command my husband/wife to be recovered by fire by force in Jesus name.*

40. *I command my children to be recovered by fire by force in the name of Jesus.*

41. *I command my health to be recovered by fire by force in Jesus name.*

42. *I command my anointing to be recovered by fire by force in the name of Jesus.*

43. *I command my dreams and visions to be recovered by fire by force in the name of Jesus from every ancestral and familiar strongman.*

PROPHETIC PRAYERS:

1. *Heavenly Father, You are the Mighty man in battle, I ask You to arise and let my enemies who have risen up against me be scattered in the name of Jesus Christ.*

2. In the name of Jesus, I pray do not let my enemies rejoice over me.

3. Heavenly father, I ask You to deliver me and my family from the spells and curses of witches and wizards in Jesus name.

4. I ask for your supernatural intervention in my life and situation in the name of Jesus. Show me your glory in my current problem Amen.

5. Heavenly father, In the name of Jesus, let all the plans, devices, plots, imaginations, conspiracy, and evil assignment of my enemies against me be destroyed by your consuming fire.

6. I cover myself and family under the precious blood of Jesus Christ and let the blood of Jesus Christ be my Passover from all evil.

7. Heavenly father, You are the Mighty man of war, I ask You to fight my enemies for me in the name of Jesus. You never lose in battle so fight my enemies for me and give me victory over the powers of darkness in Jesus name.

8. Heavenly father, You are the author and finisher of my faith. I ask You in the name of Jesus to help me finish every good thing You have started in my life. I ask You to help me finish this week, month, and year victoriously.

9. *In Jesus name, I declare and decree by faith that wherever my enemies have gathered against me let them perish in Jesus name. Wherever they have gathered against me in the air, water, sea, rivers, forest, tree, coven, underground, and high places let them all catch fire and burn into ashes in Jesus name.*

10. In the name of Jesus Christ, I command every satanic plans, attacks, arrows, witchcraft, obeah, voodoo, Santeria, sorceries, hexes, curses, and divination against me to catch fire burn into ashes in the name of Jesus.

11. *In the Mighty name of Jesus Christ, I command the monitoring devices, magical mirrors, satanic antenna, crystal ball, psychic computers, satanic animals, and witchcraft pot to catch fire and burn into ashes.*

12. In the Mighty name of Jesus Christ, I plead the blood of Jesus Christ to overcome and destroy all activities of demons and witchcraft attacks against me and my family. I neutralize the powers and plans of demons and witches against me in Jesus name.

13. *In the Mighty name of Jesus Christ, I destroy by fire every witchcraft contamination and affliction over my life and body through food and water in my dream.*

14. *Heavenly father, your name is Jehovah Jireh, I ask You to provide for me and my family speedily in the name of Jesus.*

15. *By the power in the name of Jesus Christ, I break and nullify every curse from my paternal and maternal bloodline, which is operating against me in Jesus name.*

16. *Heavenly father, in the Mighty name of Jesus Christ, Let my life from this year start moving forward. I ask You to be magnified and glorified in my life this year in the name of Jesus.*

17. *Heavenly father, in the Mighty name of Jesus Christ, I ask You to deliver me from destiny destroyers. Let my soul escape from their hands and traps in Jesus name.*

18. *In the Mighty name of Jesus Christ, I command every evil plans and plot against me and my family to be reversed now.*

19. **In the name of Jesus Christ, I command every killing demons assigned against me and my family to catch fire and die.**

20. In the name of Jesus Christ, I command every stealing demon on assignment to steal from me to catch fire and die in Jesus name.

21. **In the name of Jesus Christ, I command every destroying spirit and agents on assignment against me to destroy me to catch fire and burn into ashes. I command them to die by fire in the name of Jesus.**

22. In Jesus name, I command every spirit of shame, rejection, reproach, humiliation, frustration, and disappointment to catch fire and burn into ashes.

23. I command in the name of Jesus that every strongman/strongwoman frustrating my destiny to die by fire in Jesus name.

24. I command in the name of Jesus that every witchcraft spirit opposing my destiny and glory to die by fire.

25. **In the Mighty name of Jesus Christ, I command the immediate release of my**

blessing, miracles, and breakthroughs from the camp of my enemies in Jesus name.

26. By the power of the Holy Ghost, In Jesus name I release myself and my family from every bondage and captivity of demonic and witchcraft spirits.

27. **In the Mighty name of Jesus Christ, I command the release of my blessing now into my life from the powers of darkness in the name of Jesus.**

28. I command the blessings of God to begin to manifest in my life from today in Jesus name.

29. **I command the blessing and favor of God to overtake me and my family in the name of Jesus.**

30. I erase every evil mark of witchcraft and demons against me and my family with the precious blood of Jesus Christ.

31. **I cover my body, soul, and spirit with the precious blood of Jesus Christ.**

32. I cover my family, children, spouse, house, apartment, marriage, business, finances, and

love one under the protection of the precious blood of Jesus Christ.

33. **I break the curse of delay and limitations off my life and family in the name of Jesus.**

34. I break the generational stronghold curse off my life and family in Jesus name.

35. **I command total restoration and restitution in my life and family in the name of Jesus.**

36. I command the favor and goodness of the Lord to come upon me and my household in the name of Jesus.

37. **I declare and decree marital restoration in my life in Jesus name.**

38. God of signs and wonders, perform your wonders in my life and family in Jesus name.

39. **God of wonders, I ask You to put all my enemies to complete shame and disgrace in the name of Jesus.**

40. God of signs and wonders, I ask You to favor me with double honor and breakthroughs in Jesus name

FINAL PRAYER

YOU CAN OVERCOME SATAN TODAY BY THE BLOOD OF JESUS CHRIST.
SATAN, I USE THE BLOOD OF JESUS TO OVERCOME, OVERPOWER, OVERTHROW YOU IN JESUS NAME. I SUBDUE YOU AND YOUR DEMONS BY THE BLOOD OF JESUS CHRIST IN JESUS NAME. YOU WILL NOT PREVAIL AGAINST ME AND MY FAMILY. YOUR HOLD OVER MY LIFE AND DESTINY IS BROKEN IN JESUS NAME. YOUR REIGN IN MY LIFE, DESTINY, FAMILY AND MARRIAGE IS OVERTHROWN BY THE BLOOD OF JESUS CHRIST IN JESUS NAME. YOUR OPERATIONS AND WORKS AGAINST ME AND MY FAMILY IS TOTALLY AND COMPLETELY DESTROYED AND TERMINATED IN JESUS NAME. I RECEIVE MY MIRACLE, BREAKTHROUGH, LIBERTY AND FREEDOM FROM YOUR BONDAGE IN JESUS NAME. I REBUKE AND RESIST YOU AND YOUR DEMONS BY THE BLOOD OF JESUS IN JESUS NAME.
YOU CANNOT TOUCH ME AND MY FAMILY BECAUSE WE ARE COVERED BY THE PRECIOUS BLOOD OF JESUS CHRIST WHICH DEFEATED YOU OVER 2000 YEARS AGO.
SATAN YOU ARE A LIAR AND I REFUSE TO PAY ATTENTION TO YOUR LIES.

INFORMATION ABOUT THE PRAYER LINE

Join us on **Tuesdays and Fridays** for prayers on the prayer line. We fast every Tuesdays and Fridays from 6:00 am to 6:00 pm. It is water fasting meaning you drink only water during the fast and eat when you break at 6:00 pm.

Prayer line number: **559-726-1200 and Access#: 950014#**

Hours for Prayers:
Tuesdays: 10:00 pm EST, 9:00 pm CST, 8:00 pm MST, 7:00 pm PST.
Fridays: 11:00 pm EST, 10:00 pm CST, 9:00 pm MST, 8:00 pm PST.

Scriptures for the Fasting and Prayers:
Jeremiah 33 vs. 3
Matthew 7 vs. 7
Mark 11 vs. 22 - 24
Ephesians 3 vs. 20
Ezra 8 vs. 21 and 31 -32
Isaiah 58 vs. 6
Isaiah 40 vs. 31

You can listen and join the prayer line on Internet radio:
www.blogtalkradio.com/kwaku-boachie

You can join the prayer line from outside America through my
Skype: Kayboachie
Facebook: Kay Boachie
Email: ookaku55@yahoo.com

Website for Prayer Line: www.freshfireprayer.com
Contact number: **443-975-5303**

The First week or second week of every month we have a one-week fasting and prayers to wait on the Lord. We meet regularly on the prayer line in the evening for prayer.

We have three conferences in a given year. Call and find out about when the next '**HOUR OF POWER WITH JESUS CONFERENCE**' is coming on. Conference is designed to deal with curses and strongholds talked about in this book. If you need deliverance then make arrangement and join the HOUR OF POWER CONFERENCE.

Sunday Service:
We meet every Sunday From 4:00pm to 7:00pm for prayers.
We are currently meeting at:
County Road Shopping Center:
1948 County Road, District Height, MD 20747

Please call to check our location before visiting our church.

If you want to better understand spiritual warfare and how to overcome the devil, then order a copy of the book SPIRITUAL DIAGNOSIS AND FREEDOM FROM GENERATIONAL CURSE AND STRONGHOLDS written by Brother Kay (Kwaku Boachie) and also SELF DELIVERACNE PACKAGE AND FIRE FOR FIRE PRAYERS CDS.

Go to our website: www.freshfireprayer.com and place your order or email/call for order.
Email: ookaku55@yahoo.com
Call: 443-975-5303